Tuscany Travel Guide

The Ultimate Travel Guide For Planning Your Trip To Tuscany From Florence, To Leaning Tower of Pisa, What To Do, What To Pack, Food To Try Out etc.

John Lucas

All rights reserved. No part of this publication may be reproduced, distributed, or transmitted in any form or by any means, including photocopying, recording, or other electronic or mechanical methods, without the prior written permission of the publisher, except in the case of brief quotations embodied in critical reviews and certain other noncommercial uses permitted by copyright law.

*John © **Enzo Lucas***

Table of Contents

Brief History 10

Geography of Tuscany 12

Tourists Must Know Things Before Visiting 14

Best Tuscany Touring Apps 19

    Google Maps 19

    Airbnb 19

    Trenitalia 20

    MyTaxi 20

    Yelp 20

    Duolingo 21

    Florencetown 21

    TripAdvisor 21

    Musement 22

    Booking 22

Tourist Activities in Tuscany 24

Tuscan Dialects and Language 33

Activities To Throughout The Year 43

    January 43

    February 43

    March 44

    April 44

    May 44

June	44
July	45
August	45
September	45
October	45
November	46
December	46
Tuscany Weather	**47**
Getting To Tuscany	**49**
By Plane	49
By Train	49
By Bus	50
By Car	50
Top Attractions	**51**
Florence	51
Chianti	56
Siena	60
Val d'Orcia	65
Pisa	69
Lucca	72
San Gimignano	76
Volterra	80
Montepulciano	83

    Cortona 86
Top Cuisine to Try Out 89
    Bistecca alla Fiorentina............................. 89
    Ribollita 92
    Pappa al Pomodoro 95
    Crostini 98
    Porchetta 100
    Cantucci 103
    Schiacciata alla Fiorentina 105
    Gelato 108
    Chianti wine 111
    Fagioli all'uccelletto 113
    Pappardelle 115
    Risotto alla Milanese 117
    Tagliatelle al tartufo 119
    Torta della Nonna 121
    Castagnaccio 123
    Acquacotta 125
    Cacciucco 127
Best time to visit Tuscany 129
Beaches in Tuscany 131
Traveling Essentials 133
    General Essentials 133

Hiking Essentials	135
Swimming Essentials	138
Traveling Itinerary	141
8 Days Itinerary	141
2-Week Itinerary	145
Tuscany 3 weeks Itinerary	148
Week 2: Southern Tuscany	149
Week 3: Western Tuscany	150
Visiting Tuscany On a Budget	152
Accommodation	152
Food and drink	153
Transportation	153
Sights and activities	154
Getting Around	156
Rail	156
Bus	156
Car rental	157
Taxi	157
Bicycle	157
Walking	158
Shared Shuttle Bus Services	158
Shopping for Souvenirs	159
Leather goods	159

- Pottery 159
- Wine and Olive Oil 160
- Jewelry 160
- Clothing 161
- Food 161
- Art 161
- Souvenir shops 162
- Markets 162
- Where to buy 162

Tips for buying souvenirs in Tuscany 163
- Be mindful of false things 163
- Negotiate prices 163
- Buy local items 163
- Take your time 164

Tour Package Options 165
Tourist Safety Tips 168
Festival and Culture 172

8

Brief History

Tuscany is a region in central Italy recognized for its magnificent scenery, rich history, and artistic heritage. The region has a vast and diversified history that spans over two thousand years and has been shaped by different civilizations and cultures, including the Etruscans, Romans, and Renaissance.

The Etruscans were one of the earliest civilizations in Tuscany and left behind a rich legacy, including the cities of Florence, Pisa, and Siena. The Roman Empire advanced into Tuscany in the 3rd century BC and the region became an important center of trade, agriculture, and culture. During the Roman period, Tuscany saw the creation of several remarkable structures, including the Amphitheater of Florence and the Roman Theatre of Fiesole.

In the Middle Ages, Tuscany was divided into various city-states, each with its own culture and history. Florence, for example, became a center of commerce and the birthplace of the Renaissance. The Renaissance was a period of immense cultural, scientific, and creative achievement and witnessed the birth of notable artists and intellectuals such as Leonardo da Vinci, Michelangelo, and Galileo Galilei.

Tuscany was also a prominent actor in the political and economic life of Italy throughout the Renaissance. The great city-state of Florence, under the control of the Medici family, became one of the wealthiest and most prominent towns in Europe. The Medici family patronized many of the great artists and philosophers of the time and helped to promote the ideals of the Renaissance throughout Europe.

Tuscany was also the birthplace of the Italian language, which became the standard language of the country after the unification of Italy in the 19th century. During this time, Tuscany played a major part in the struggle for Italian independence and was home to several prominent political figures, including Giuseppe Garibaldi.

It is a territory with a rich and diversified history that has been shaped by the Etruscans, Romans, Renaissance, and many other civilizations and cultures. Today, Tuscany is a renowned tourist destination, attracting millions of people each year with its gorgeous landscapes, rich cultural legacy, and world-famous cities. Whether you're interested in art, or architecture, or simply want to relax in the countryside, Tuscany has something to offer everyone.

Geography of Tuscany

Tuscany is famed for its gorgeous rolling hills, stunning scenery, medieval cities, and world-famous art and architecture. Tuscany covers an area of over 23,000 square kilometers and is home to around 3.7 million persons.

The landscape of Tuscany is characterized by the Apennine Mountains which stretch through the region from north to south. These mountains provide a magnificent background to the region and are perfect for outdoor activities such as hiking and mountain riding. The region is also noted for its fertile plains, which are used for agriculture and are interspersed with vineyards, olive trees, and rolling hills.

The Arno River runs through Tuscany and is one of the most important waterways in the region. The river is used for irrigation and is also a popular place for water sports such as kayaking and rafting. The coastal sections of Tuscany are famed for their magnificent beaches and crystal-clear waters, making them a favorite destination for sun-seekers and beach enthusiasts.

Tuscany is also home to several historic cities, including Florence, Pisa, and Siena. Florence is one of the most recognized towns in the world and is known for its rich cultural heritage, breathtaking architecture, and world-class art museums. Pisa is a prominent tourist destination for its medieval architecture and historic sites. Siena is a fascinating medieval city with a rich cultural past and is noted for its stunning hilltop setting and stunning panoramic vistas.

Tuscany is also famed for its rich culinary legacy and is home to some of the best food and wine in the world. The region is famous for its traditional cuisines such as Ribollita, a substantial vegetable soup, and Bistecca alla Fiorentina, a superb beef dish. Tuscany is also famed for its wine and is home to several world-renowned vineyards, including Chianti, Brunello di Montalcino, and Vino Nobile di Montepulciano.

Must Know Things Before Visiting

When arranging a journey to Tuscany, here are some crucial things to bear in mind:

Getting around: Tuscany has a great public transit infrastructure, including trains, buses, and taxis, making it easy to get around. However, if you're planning on touring the countryside and tiny villages, a rental car is advisable.

Accommodation: Tuscany provides a choice of accommodation alternatives, from budget-friendly hostels to opulent five-star hotels. Many guests opt to stay in agriturismo, which are typical Tuscan farmhouses that have been turned into guesthouses.

Food and wine: Tuscany is recognized for its wonderful cuisine, including substantial soups, pasta dishes, and grilled meats. The region is also home to some of Italy's most famous wine districts, including Chianti, and Brunello di Montalcino. Be sure to try a few local foods and drinks throughout your vacation.

Sights to see: Tuscany is home to several historic cities and towns, including Florence, Siena, Pisa, and Lucca. In addition, the region is filled with attractive villages and rolling hills, making it the perfect destination for scenic drives and hikes.

Art and Architecture: Tuscany is recognized for its artistic heritage, with many of the world's most famous pieces of art and architecture located in the region. Florence, in particular, is a treasure mine of artistic marvels, including Michelangelo's David, Botticelli's Birth of Venus, and the Uffizi Gallery.

Language: Although Italian is the official language of Tuscany, many locals speak English, especially in tourist areas. However, it's always a good idea to learn a few fundamental words in Italian to help you get by.

Money: The currency used in Tuscany is the Euro. Credit and debit cards are generally accepted, but it's always a good idea to keep some cash on hand for smaller purchases and tips.

Safety: Tuscany is typically a safe place to visit, but it's always a good idea to remain careful of your surroundings, especially in popular tourist areas. Take the standard steps to secure your possessions and be wary of pickpocketing.

Respect local customs: Tuscany is a traditional, conservative region, and it's necessary to respect local customs and traditions. Dress modestly, especially when visiting religious locations, and avoid loud and disruptive behavior in public areas.

Shopping: Tuscany is recognized for its artisanal items, including leather goods, ceramics, jewelry, and textiles. Many of these objects are unique to the region and make fantastic mementos or gifts. Be sure to visit local markets and boutiques to locate the ideal thing to take home.

Festivals and events: Tuscany is host to several festivals and events throughout the year, including the Palio di Siena horse race, the Florence Wine Festival, and the Luminara di San Ranieri in Pisa. Check local calendars to see if any events are happening during your visit and consider attending for a unique and unforgettable experience.

Photography: Tuscany is one of the most picturesque places in the world, with its undulating hills, medieval cities, and lovely villages. Whether you're a professional photographer or just enjoy taking photos, make sure to bring your camera and take advantage of the many opportunities to create great images.

Sustainability: Tuscany is an area that prioritizes sustainability and eco-friendly activities. Many hotels and guesthouses have adopted sustainable tourism, allowing guests the opportunity to experience Tuscany in a responsible and environmentally conscientious way. If you're interested in sustainable travel, make sure to seek out eco-friendly accommodations throughout your vacation.

Rural Life: Tuscany is also famed for its rural life, with magnificent farms and vineyards dotting the countryside. If you're interested in experiencing the traditional way of life in Tuscany, consider visiting a local farm or taking a guided tour of a vineyard. You'll have the opportunity to learn about the history, culture, and traditions of the region and try some of the local cuisine and wine.

Beaches: Tuscany is not only famed for its rolling hills and old cities but also for its magnificent coastline. The region is home to numerous magnificent beaches, including the famed Viareggio, Castiglione della Pescaia, and Cala Violina. If you're looking for a break from the city, consider visiting one of these beaches to soak up the sun and enjoy the Mediterranean Sea.

Museums: Tuscany is also home to many museums, showcasing the rich history, art, and culture of the region. Some of the most popular museums include the Museo Nazionale del Bargello in Florence, the Museo dell'Opera del Duomo in Pisa, and the Museo Civico di San Gimignano. Whether you're interested in art, history, or local culture, there's a museum in Tuscany that will suit your interests.

Spa towns: Tuscany is famed for its spa towns, including Montecatini Terme, Chianciano Terme, and Bagni di Lucca. These cities offer visitors the opportunity to rest and refresh in natural thermal spas, taking advantage of the medicinal effects of the hot springs. If you're looking to pamper yourself on your visit to Tuscany, consider visiting one of these spa towns.

Religious sites: Tuscany is also home to several religious sites, including cathedrals, churches, and monasteries. Some of the most prominent religious sites in Tuscany include the Cathedral of Santa Maria del Fiore in Florence, the Pisa Baptistery, and the Monastery of San Galgano. If you're interested in religious history and architecture, be sure to visit a few of these locations during your stay in Tuscany.

This region offers something for everyone, from art and history to natural beauty and outdoor activities. With careful planning and regard for the local culture and customs, you're sure to have a memorable and enriching experience in this lovely location.

Best Tuscany Touring Apps

As a visitor visiting Tuscany, you can make the most of your trip by using a few crucial smartphone applications to help you plan and manage your trips.

Google Maps

Google Maps is a must-have for any visitor, no matter where you are traveling. This software will help you travel to Tuscany with ease, offering you turn-by-turn directions to your selected destinations. It also allows you to search for restaurants, stores, and attractions near you, so you can make the most of your time in Tuscany. You can also save maps offline, so you can utilize them without an online connection.

Airbnb

Airbnb is a terrific tool to uncover unique and economical housing options in Tuscany. From apartments to villas to treehouses, you'll discover a selection of accommodations to choose from that suit your budget and vacation style. You may use the app to book and communicate with your host, assuring a seamless and hassle-free stay.

Trenitalia

Trenitalia is the official app of the Italian national railway operator and gives information on train timetables and ticket rates. If you're traveling throughout Tuscany, trains are a simple and cost-effective method to get about, and this software makes it easy to plan and book your journeys.

MyTaxi

MyTaxi is a cab booking software that makes it easy to navigate Tuscany without having to worry about navigating public transportation or driving. Simply enter your pickup and drop-off destinations, and the app will find you a taxi in the neighborhood. You can pay for your transport through the app, and you can also evaluate your driver, assuring a high-quality service for future passengers.

Yelp

Yelp is an app that allows you to search for restaurants, pubs, cafes, and other food venues in Tuscany. You may read reviews from other tourists and residents, see images, and get directions to the destination you're searching for. The app also provides recommendations depending on your location, so you can easily discover a place to dine or drink near.

Duolingo

If you're traveling to Tuscany and want to learn some Italian, Duolingo is a terrific program to help you get started. With classes geared to teach you the essentials of the language, you'll be able to speak with locals and travel around with more ease. You may also use the app to practice your Italian while on the road.

Florencetown

Florencetown is a website that provides a thorough tour to Florence. The website gives information on museums, churches, monuments, and other tourist attractions, and also offers walking tours, bike excursions, and cookery workshops. You can also get information on local events, festivals, and markets.

Website: Florencetown.com

TripAdvisor

TripAdvisor owns a website and app that provides information about destinations, sights, and restaurants in Tuscany. You may read reviews from other travelers, view images, and book appointments directly from the app. The app also includes maps, tour and activity suggestions.

Website: TripAdvisor.com

Musement

Musement is a website that helps you organize and book tours, events, and tickets for attractions in Tuscany. From culinary courses and wine tastings to guided tours of the iconic Uffizi Gallery and the Vatican, you'll find a variety of experiences to select from. You may schedule and pay for your activities straight from the website, making it easier to plan your itinerary and save time.

Website: Musement.com

Booking

Booking is a popular online platform for travellers visiting Tuscany or anyplace else in the world, offering a wide selection of accommodations including hotels, apartments, villas, and bed and breakfasts. The platform makes it easy for travellers to compare pricing, read reviews from past guests, and book rooms quickly and securely. Booking.com also offers special bargains and discounts, making it an enticing option for budget-conscious tourists. To utilize the platform, simply enter your location and travel dates and browse through the various possibilities. You may filter results by price, location, and other factors to discover the perfect place to stay. With Booking.com, you can be secure in your travel plans and enjoy a stress-free journey to Tuscany.

Website: Booking.com

These are wonderful mobile programs that you can download from your mobile App Store for IOS devices and websites that will help you make the most of your trip to Tuscany. From navigating the region to locating the best places to eat, drink and stay, these apps will make your trip more fun and stress-free. Whether you're a first-time visitor or a seasoned tourist, be sure to download these applications.

Tourist Activities in Tuscany

There are plenty of activities for travelers to do in Tuscany, ranging from seeing historical sites to experiencing local cuisine and wines. Here are some of the most popular activities that travelers can experience in Tuscany:

Visit the Cities of Florence, Siena, and Pisa

- These cities are located in Tuscany and are recognized for their rich history, architecture, and art. Florence is home to various museums, notably the Uffizi Gallery, which holds some of the world's most famous paintings and sculptures. Siena is a lovely ancient town that is famous for its Palio horse race and its gorgeous Piazza del Campo. Pisa is best renowned for its Leaning Tower, but it is also home to several other outstanding architectural structures, such as the Cathedral and Baptistery.

Explore the Chianti Wine Region

- Chianti is one of the most famous wine areas in the world, and it is located in the heart of Tuscany. Wine connoisseurs can visit the vineyards, taste the wines, and learn about the local winemaking traditions. There are also various wine tours available that take guests through the vineyards and to some of the most famous wineries in the region.

Take a Hot Air Balloon Ride

- One of the greatest ways to observe Tuscany's rolling hills and stunning scenery is from the air. There are various hot air balloon businesses that provide rides over the Tuscany region, affording spectacular views of the countryside below.

Visit the Thermal Baths

- Tuscany is home to various thermal baths, which are hot springs that are famed for their medicinal effects. Tourists can visit these baths to rest and rejuvenate, and there are several spa resorts in the region that provide a variety of treatments and services.

Walk the Via Francigena

- The Via Francigena is an old pilgrimage road that extends from Canterbury, England, to Rome. A segment of this path travels through Tuscany, and tourists can follow this trail to see some of the most beautiful and historic sights in the region.

Visit Cinque Terre

- Cinque Terre is a seaside region in Tuscany that is noted for its five beautiful villages and its stunning surroundings. Visitors can trek along the trails that connect the settlements, swim in the pristine waters of the Ligurian Sea, and experience the local food.

Visit the Medieval Castles

- Tuscany is home to various historic castles that date back to the Middle Ages. Tourists can visit these castles to learn about the local history and to witness the amazing architectural features that have been preserved over the years.

Go Truffle Hunting

- Tuscany is famous for its truffles, and there are various truffle hunting tours available in the region. Visitors can learn about the truffle-hunting process, and even try their hand at hunting for these uncommon and precious fungi.

Take a Cooking Class

- Tuscany is recognized for its exquisite cuisine, and there are various cooking programs offered that teach guests how to prepare classic Tuscan meals. Participants can learn about the local ingredients and cooking skills, and they can try the dishes that they prepare.

Visit the Beaches

- Tuscany is home to several gorgeous beaches, and visitors may spend a day relaxing and swimming in the Mediterranean Sea. There are also various water sports available, including snorkeling, kayaking, and windsurfing

Visit the Museums

- Tuscany is home to various museums, including the Accademia Gallery in Florence, which holds Michelangelo's iconic statue of David. The Palazzo Pitti in Florence is also a prominent museum that shows an impressive collection of Renaissance paintings and sculptures.

Take a Bike Tour

- Tuscany is a terrific destination for riding, and there are various bike tours available that take visitors through the rolling hills and gorgeous scenery. This is a terrific way to view the countryside at a leisurely pace and to get some exercise at the same time.

Visit the Markets

- Tuscany is home to various markets, including the famed San Lorenzo market in Florence, which is one of the largest open-air markets in

Italy. Visitors can peruse the vendors, eat the local food, and buy souvenirs and gifts.

Attend a Festival

- Tuscany is host to various events, including the famed Palio horse race in Siena. Visitors can experience the local culture and traditions by attending one of these festivals and enjoying the local food, music, and entertainment.

Hiking & Trekking

- This Region offers a plethora of chances for outdoor enthusiasts to experience the region's magnificent scenery on foot. From short walks to strenuous hikes, there are pathways for all levels of fitness and expertise. The Parco Nazionale delle Foreste Casentinesi, Monte Falterona e Campigna, the Parco Naturale dell'Uccellina, the Parco Naturale della Maremma, and the Chianti hills are also popular hiking locations.

Biking

- Tuscany is an excellent destination for cycling, with its rolling hills and calm roads giving a tough and scenic journey. The Chianti hills, Val d'Orcia, and the Maremma are popular cycling destinations, offering miles of peaceful roads and stunning scenery. There are also bike rental facilities accessible, so tourists may quickly rent a bike and hit the trails.

Wine tasting

- Tuscany is famed for its wine, and what better way to enjoy it than to go on a wine tour? The region is home to many vineyards and wineries, many of which provide tastings and tours. Visitors can sample the local wines and learn about the history and tradition of wine-making in Tuscany.

Wildlife watching

- Tuscany is home to a vast and diversified array of wildlife, including deer, wild boar, and birds of prey. Visitors can embark on guided wildlife tours or join a nature reserve to witness these animals in their natural habitat.

Swimming and sunbathing

- Tuscany is home to some of Italy's most magnificent beaches, with crystal-clear waters and sandy shorelines. Some popular beach sites are Castiglione Della Pescaia, Marina di Grosseto, and Punta Ala.

Culinary tours

- Tuscany is recognized for its exquisite cuisine, and visitors may revel in the region's culinary legacy by going on a culinary tour. These excursions often include visits to local markets and farms, as well as cookery courses, where guests can learn how to prepare classic Tuscan cuisine.

Art and architecture

- Tuscany is home to some of the world's most famous art and architecture, including masterpieces by Leonardo da Vinci, Michelangelo, and many others. Visitors can see the region's many museums, churches, and palaces, which are rich with treasures and breathtaking architecture.

Olive grove tours

- Tuscany is famed for its olive oil, and visitors may learn about the production of this key ingredient by embarking on an olive grove tour. These trips often include visits to local farms and groves, where you may learn about the history of olive oil production in Tuscany, and watch the process of harvesting and pressing the olives.

Scenic drives

- Tuscany is full of gorgeous and attractive roads that give stunning views of the countryside. Visitors can rent a car and explore the region at their own speed, stopping to take in the gorgeous landscape and visiting tiny communities along the way. Some popular picturesque roads are the Strada Degli Dei and the Chiantigiana road.

Water activities

- Tuscany is home to various lakes and rivers that offer a range of water sports, such as kayaking, rafting, and stand-up paddleboarding. Lake Trasimeno, Lake Bolsena, and the Arno River are excellent places for water activities.

Rock climbing

- Tuscany offers a range of climbing and bouldering options, with its stunning cliffs and outcrops. The Grotta del Vento and Monte Pisano are renowned climbing sites, offering routes for climbers of all levels of experience.

Fishing

- Tuscany is home to various rivers, lakes, and coastal waters that offer good fishing opportunities. Whether you're an expert angler or just looking to try something new, fishing in Tuscany is a pleasant and gratifying activity.

Horse riding

- Tuscany is a wonderful place for horse riding, with its rolling hills and lovely landscape creating the perfect environment for a leisurely ride. Visitors can join a guided tour, embark on a horse excursion, or even take a horse riding instruction.

Tuscan Dialects and Language

The official language spoken in Tuscany is Italian, although there are also various regional dialects that are peculiar to the area.

The most notable of these dialects is termed "Tuscan," which is a variety of Italian that has been impacted by the area's distinctive history and culture. Tuscan is noted for its particular pronunciation, vocabulary, and syntax, and it is still extensively spoken in the region today. For example, the Tuscan accent is defined by its gentle and lyrical intonation, and it has a slower pace compared to standard Italian.

There are also various more dialects that are spoken in Tuscany, such as "Fiorentino" and "Livornese." These dialects are largely spoken in the cities of Florence and Livorno, respectively, and they have their own distinct language traits and cultural nuances.

For travelers visiting Tuscany, it is vital to understand that while many locals do speak some degree of English, it is not as extensively spoken as in some other parts of Italy or Europe. Additionally, many older generations of Tuscans may not speak English at all, so it is a good idea to brush up on your Italian or learn some crucial words before your trip.

However, despite the distinctions in dialect and language, the people of Tuscany are generally quite pleasant and inviting to guests, and they are always happy to help. Whether you are looking for local advice, directions, or just someone to chat with, the Tuscans are always happy to provide a hand.

It is also worth adding that Tuscany is famed for its rich literary and cultural past, and this is reflected in the local language and dialects as well. For example, the Tuscan dialect has been utilized by many notable Italian poets, writers, and artists throughout history, notably Dante Alighieri, who composed the "Divine Comedy" in the Tuscan dialect.

Another important element of the dialect is its influence on the Italian language as a whole. The dialect was utilized as the basis for the modern Italian language, and it has played a vital influence in determining the way Italian is spoken and written today. This is why Tuscan is sometimes referred to as the "Mother of the Italian language."

Visitors can also experience the local language and dialects through the many festivals and events, such as the yearly "Festa Della Rificolona," which is held in Florence. This festival is dedicated to the Virgin Mary and comprises processions, parades, and Tuscan songs and dances, all of which are performed in the local dialect.

Many local restaurants and cafes in Tuscany also offer menus and signage in both Italian and the local dialect, providing guests with a rare opportunity to experience the local language and culture first-hand.

The language spoken in Tuscany is Italian, but there are also various regional dialects that are distinctive to the area. Whether you are an Italian speaker or not, the local people are always pleased to help, and the dialects and languages are an intrinsic part of the region's rich cultural legacy. Make sure to embrace the local language and dialects, and you are sure to have a genuinely authentic and amazing experience.

Common phrases you can certainly hear from locals and use as well.

Here are some frequent phrases that travelers visiting might expect to hear from locals and what they mean:

"Ciao" - Hello

This is the most common greeting in Italy and is used as both a casual hello and a goodbye.

"Come stai?" - How are you?

This is a friendly way of asking someone how they are doing.

"Buongiorno" - Good morning

This is a polite greeting to use in the morning, similar to saying "good morning" in English.

"Buonasera" - Good evening

This is a polite greeting to use in the evening, similar to saying "good evening" in English.

"Grazie" - Thank you

This is the Italian word for thank you, which is used to express gratitude for something.

"Per favore" - Please

This is the Italian word for please, which is used to ask for something in a polite way.

"Scusa" - Excuse me

This is used to get someone's attention or to apologize for something.

"Mi dispiace" - I'm sorry

This is used to apologize for something, similar to saying "I'm sorry" in English.

"Dov'è?" - Where is?

This is used to ask where something or someone is located.

"Quanto costa?" - How much does it cost?

This is used to ask the price of something.

"Parla inglese?" - Do you speak English?

This is used to ask if someone speaks English.

"Non capisco" - I don't understand"

This is used to express that you don't understand what someone is saying.

"Sì" - Yes

This is the Italian word for yes, which is used to express agreement or affirmation.

"No" - No

This is the Italian word for no, which is used to express disagreement or negation.

"Vino rosso" - Red wine

This is used to order red wine, which is a popular drink in Tuscany.

"Bella giornata" - Beautiful day

This is used to describe a beautiful day or to express appreciation for the weather.

"Che delizia" - What a delight

This is used to express how delicious or enjoyable something is.

"Questo è fantastico" - This is fantastic

This is used to describe something that is fantastic or amazing.

"Siamo qui per divertirci" - We are here to have fun

This is used to express the intention of having a good time or enjoying oneself.

"Non mi piace" - I don't like it

This is used to express that you don't like something.

"Che bella cosa" - What a beautiful thing

This is used to express admiration for something that is beautiful or special.

"Non me ne importa niente" - I don't care about it

This is used to express that you don't care about something or have no interest in it.

"Sto andando" - I'm going

This is used to express that you are on your way to somewhere.

"Fa niente" - It doesn't matter

This is used to express that something is not important or has no consequence.

"Andiamo a vedere" - Let's go see

This is used to suggest that you go and see something, often used to suggest visiting a place or attraction.

"Perché no?" - Why not?

This is used to ask why something shouldn't happen or be done.

"Fa presto" - Hurry up

This is used to encourage someone to move more quickly or to get something done faster.

"Come va?" - How is it going?

This is used to ask someone how they are doing or how things are going for them.

"E allora?" - And then?

This is used to ask what will happen next or to continue a conversation.

"Non mi interessa" - I'm not interested

This is used to express that you have no interest in something.

"Che bella persona" - What a beautiful person

This is used to express admiration for someone who is beautiful, kind, or special in some way.

"A domani" - See you tomorrow

This is used to say goodbye and express the intention of seeing someone tomorrow.

"Che cosa fai?" - What are you doing?

This is used to ask someone what they are currently doing.

"Perché?" - Why?

This is used to ask for an explanation or reason for something.

"Come stai?" - How are you?

This is used to ask someone how they are feeling or how their day is going.

"Mi piace" - I like it

This is used to express enjoyment or appreciation for something.

"Non ti preoccupare" - Don't worry

This is used to reassure someone or to tell them not to be concerned about something.

"Dai!" - Come on!

This is used to encourage someone to do something or to show excitement about something.

You can use the recommended "**Duolingo app**" to learn more about the Italian language.

These terms and phrases are only some of the many linguistic nuances that you will meet in Tuscany. Whether you are traveling for the first time or are a seasoned tourist, understanding a few of these expressions can help you to connect with the locals and immerse yourself more fully in the Tuscan culture and way of life.

Activities To Throughout The Year

Tuscany offers a range of activities to tourists all year round. Some of the most popular ones are:

January

-Visit Florence at the Epiphany (January 6th), to witness the traditional "Calcio Storico Fiorentino" (Historical Florentine Football), a historical reenactment of the sport performed in the Renaissance.

-Warm up in the hot springs of Saturnia.

-Attend the "Fiera di Sant'Antonio Abate" (St. Anthony's Fair), a traditional livestock fair in Arezzo.

February

-Celebrate Carnevale (Carnival), with parades and masked parties in Viareggio and Florence.

-Visit the "Fiera Internazionale dell'Artigianato" (International Craft Fair) in Florence.

March

-Take part in the Easter celebrations in Florence, with the "Scoppio del Carro" (Explosion of the Cart) being a highlight.

-Visit the tulip and iris gardens in the countryside.

April

-Enjoy the gorgeous scenery of Tuscany in springtime.

-Visit the "Fiera di Primavera" (Spring Fair) in Florence, displaying local arts and crafts.

May

-See the wonderful flowering of the countryside with a leisurely drive or bike ride.

-Attend the "Calcio in Costume" (Football in Costume), a medieval football game in costume in Florence.

June

-Visit the beaches of the Tuscan coast, such as Forte Dei Marmi or Marina di Pietrasanta.

-Explore the "Festa Dei Ceri" (Feast of the Candles) in Gubbio, a medieval procession with candles.

July

-Experience the "Fiera di San Giovanni" (St. John's Fair) in Florence, with food and artisan vendors, live music, and fireworks.

-Take part in the "Palio di Siena" horse race in Siena.

August

-Visit the medieval city of Pienza for the "Fiera Nazionale Dei Formaggi" (National Cheese Fair).

-Enjoy the "Notte Bianca" (White Night) in Florence, with art displays, concerts, and open-air festivities.

September

-Visit the "Fiera di San Matteo" (St. Matthew's Fair) in Florence, promoting local produce and crafts.

-Take part in the "Fiera Della Zolfina" (Zolfina Fair) in Castelnuovo Berardenga, promoting local wine and food.

October

-Attend the "Fiera di San Giovanni" (St. John's Fair) at Certaldo, including medieval reenactments and street performers.

-Visit the "Fiera Delle Sagre" (Fair of the Festivals) in Greve in Chianti, highlighting local food and wine.

November

-Visit the "Fiera di Sant'Andrea" (St. Andrew's Fair) in Arezzo, displaying local arts and crafts.

-Enjoy the "Fiera di San Martino" (St. Martin's Fair) in Florence, featuring food and wine kiosks.

December

Visit the "Mercatino di Natale" (Christmas Market) in Florence, featuring traditional gifts and food stalls.

Tuscany Weather

The weather of Tuscany is considered to be one of the best in Europe, with warm, sunny summers and mild, rainy winters.

Summer months in Tuscany, from June through August, are pleasant and sunny, with average temperatures ranging from 25°C to 30°C. July and August are the hottest months, with occasional heat waves reaching 35°C or higher. This is the finest time for tourists to visit Tuscany, as the weather is perfect for outdoor activities such as sunbathing, hiking, and swimming in the Mediterranean.

Autumn, from September to November, is a transition phase between summer and winter, with temperatures gradually decreasing and rains rising. The weather during this season can be mild or cool, depending on the day, with occasional bursts of warm sunshine. This is a good time to visit Tuscany if you prefer milder temperatures and wish to escape the crowds of summer tourists.

Winter months, from December through February, are normally warm, with temperatures ranging from 8°C to 12°C. There is also a higher risk of rain and overcast days, but the location is nevertheless popular with travelers who prefer the peace and quiet of the off-season. Winters are also the season when Tuscany's famous vineyards come to life, with wine tasting and harvest festivities taking place around the region.

Spring, from March to May, is another transition phase, with warm temperatures and occasional showers. This is a popular season to visit Tuscany, especially in May, when the countryside is in bloom and wildflowers carpet the hillsides. It is also an excellent time to explore the cities, as the weather is comfortable for sightseeing and outdoor activities.

Regardless of the season, Tuscany's weather is impacted by the region's location, wedged between the Tyrrhenian Sea and the Apennine Mountains. This results in microclimates, with certain locations being warmer or cooler than others, so it's essential to check the local weather forecast before organizing your route.

Tuscany's weather is one of the great attractions of the region, with warm, sunny summers, mild and rainy winters, and agreeable temperatures during the transition seasons of autumn and spring. Whether you are wanting to relax on the beach, explore the countryside, or soak up the culture of Tuscany's lovely villages, you will find the perfect weather conditions to meet your needs.

Getting To Tuscany

Various ways to get to Tuscany.

By Plane

The primary airport in Tuscany is Florence's Peretola Airport (FLR), which is located about 6 kilometers from the city center. This airport is well-connected to key cities in Europe, including London, Paris, and Munich, making it a convenient option for foreign tourists. Once you arrive at the airport, you can take a cab, bus, or train to reach your final destination in Tuscany.

Another airport in Tuscany is Pisa's International Airport or Galileo Galilei Airport (PSA), which is located about 12 km from the city of Pisa. This airport is also well-connected to major European cities, and from here, you may take a train or bus to explore other parts of Tuscany.

By Train

If you are already in Italy, one of the most convenient and scenic ways to go to Tuscany is by rail. The primary railway station in Tuscany is Florence's Santa Maria Novella Station, which is connected to the major towns in Italy, such as Rome, Milan, and Venice. From here, you can use regional trains to visit smaller towns in Tuscany, including Siena, Lucca, and Pisa.

By Bus

If you prefer to travel by bus, you can take one of the many regional buses that connect the major cities in Tuscany, such as Florence, Pisa, and Siena. The buses are run by numerous firms and offer a quick and cost-effective means to travel across the region.

By Car

If you have your own car, driving is a practical method to travel to Tuscany, especially if you plan to explore the region on your own. There are various roadways that connect Tuscany to other parts of Italy, such as the A1 motorway, which stretches from Milan to Rome and passes through Florence. It is vital to know that driving in Tuscany can be tough, especially in the more rural parts, where roads are small and winding.

Top Attractions

Tuscany is famed for its rich cultural legacy, breathtaking landscapes, and stunning buildings. Some of the prominent tourist destinations in Tuscany are:

Florence

Florence, the birthplace of the Renaissance, is one of the most recognizable cities in Italy. Known for its rich cultural legacy, artistic wonders, and architectural marvels, Florence attracts millions of tourists every year. The center of the city is Piazza del Duomo, where the famed Cathedral of Santa Maria del Fiore is located. The cathedral, also known as the Duomo, is a wonder of Gothic architecture and is noted for its huge dome, which was constructed by Filippo Brunelleschi. The Cathedral's terrace gives a panoramic view of the city and is a popular tourist site.

Next to the Duomo lies the Baptistery of San Giovanni, a masterpiece of Romanesque construction. The Baptistery is famed for its bronze doors, especially the "Gates of Paradise" by Lorenzo Ghiberti.

The city's most famous museum, the Uffizi Gallery, exhibits a collection of treasures from the Renaissance, including works by Leonardo da Vinci, Michelangelo, Raphael, and Botticelli. The gallery is housed in a lovely palazzo overlooking the Arno River and is a must-visit for art aficionados.

The Ponte Vecchio, the oldest bridge in Florence, is also a renowned tourist attraction. The bridge is lined with gold and jewelry shops and is a unique aspect of the city's medieval architecture.

Florence is also home to the famous Accademia Gallery, where Michelangelo's David statue is displayed.

The statue is one of the most famous works of art in the world and is a symbol of Renaissance humanism and ideal beauty.

Another popular tourist location is the Palazzo Pitti, a splendid Renaissance palace that was originally the residence of the Medici family. The palace is now a museum and includes various art collections, notably the Gallery of Modern Art.

The city's principal square, Piazza Della Signoria, is a popular gathering place surrounded by historic buildings, notably the Palazzo Vecchio, the town hall of Florence. The square is also home to several renowned sculptures, including a replica of Michelangelo's David monument.

For a more leisurely experience, guests can meander around the Boboli Gardens, located behind the Pitti Palace. The gardens give a calm getaway from the hectic city and offer spectacular views of Florence and the neighboring hills.

In addition to its cultural legacy, Florence is also famed for its gastronomy. Traditional Tuscan foods, such as pasta with meat sauce, Ribollita soup, and the famous bistecca alla fiorentina, can be found in local trattorias and restaurants. The city is also famed for its gelato, which can be bought in shops across the city.

There are many more things to see and do in Florence. For example, the church of Santa Maria Novella is one of the city's largest and most magnificent churches, with a breathtaking front and interior. The church is home to various masterpieces of Renaissance art, including frescoes by Domenico Ghirlandaio.

The Basilica of San Lorenzo is another must-see location for travelers to Florence. This is the city's principal church and is recognized for its spectacular architecture, notably its pulpit by Donatello and its Laurentian Library, which houses a collection of manuscripts and literature from the Middle Ages and the Renaissance.

For people interested in science and medicine, the Museum of the History of Science is located in the city's old market hall. The museum includes a variety of scientific instruments, including Galileo's telescope and other artifacts that depict the history of science and technology in Florence.

For those who adore shopping, the marketplaces of Florence are a must-visit. The San Lorenzo market, for example, is a vibrant and colorful market selling anything from leather items to souvenirs. The neighboring Mercato Centrale, meantime, is a food market that offers a wide choice of local delicacies and products.

Another popular shopping area is the Piazza del Mercato Nuovo, which is famed for its colorful market stalls and street performers. Here, tourists may find a choice of souvenirs and trinkets, as well as leather items and apparel.

Florence is a city that offers a plethora of cultural and historical activities, as well as possibilities for shopping, dining, and leisure. Whether you are interested in art, history, or science, or simply want to relax and appreciate the city's beauty and charm, Florence is a place that should not be missed.

Chianti

Chianti is a wine-producing region located in the middle section of Tuscany. It is noted for producing one of Italy's most popular wines, Chianti Classico, which is a combination of Sangiovese grapes and other red wine types. The name "Chianti" has been used to characterize this region and its wine for hundreds of years, and it has become synonymous with high-quality Tuscan wine.

The Chianti wine-producing region is separated into various sub-zones, each with its own particular traits and wine-making traditions. Chianti Classico is the most famous sub-zone and is considered the birthplace of the Chianti wine. It is located in the heart of Tuscany and is noted for its undulating hills, vineyards, and olive orchards. The wine produced here is known for its beautiful crimson color, rich flavor, and good tannic structure.

Chianti Classico wine must meet stringent production standards to be designated as such. The wine must be prepared from a minimum of 80% Sangiovese grapes, with the remaining 20% made up of other red wine types. The grapes must be farmed in the Chianti Classico region, and the wine must be matured for a minimum of 12 months before release. The result is a wine with a distinctive and recognized flavor profile, which has made Chianti Classico one of the most popular and well-regarded wines in the world.

Visitors to Chianti can experience the region's wine culture by visiting one of the many wineries in the area. Many of these vineyards offer guided tours, tastings, and the ability to purchase wine straight from the source. Some vineyards also offer the possibility to stay on the site, allowing tourists to immerse themselves in the wine-making culture and receive a true sense of Tuscany.

In addition to the wineries, Chianti is also home to a variety of lovely ancient villages and hilltop towns. These villages, such as Castellina in Chianti, Radda in Chianti, and Gaiole in Chianti, are rich in history and provide visitors with a look into life in Tuscany centuries ago. Visitors can meander through the small streets, enjoy the ancient architecture, and stop at one of the many cafes or restaurants for a sample of local food.

It's also home to some of Tuscany's most stunning landscapes, and visitors can explore the rolling hills, vineyards, and olive groves on foot, by bike, or even by horse. There are many recognized trails and paths through the countryside, making it easier for visitors to discover the beauty of the region. For those who want a more structured experience, there are also scheduled tours available, which generally include stops at vineyards, villages, and other features of the area.

Chianti is a must-visit location for anybody interested in wine, history, or Tuscan culture. The region's blend of rolling hills, picturesque villages, and superb cuisine make it an ideal spot for a peaceful holiday. Whether you are a wine enthusiast or simply a lover of good cuisine and gorgeous surroundings, Chianti has something to offer. With its ancient wine-making legacy, tourists may learn about the history and process of making Chianti Classico and sample some of the best wines the region has to offer. Whether you prefer to stay in a traditional Tuscan villa, a warm bed, and breakfast, or a stylish hotel, there is a wide choice of lodging options available to suit all interests and budgets.

So, when arranging your trip to Tuscany, be sure to put Chianti on your agenda. Whether you are interested in trying the region's famous wines, touring its beautiful villages, or simply taking in the breathtaking vistas of the Tuscan countryside, Chianti has something to offer. With its rich history, warm hospitality, and world-class cuisine, Chianti is a must-visit destination for anybody wishing to enjoy the finest of Tuscany.

Siena

Siena is a magnificent city famed for its rich history, stunning architecture, and art. Siena attracts millions of tourists every year, and it's easy to see why. Here's a thorough guide to help you make the most of your visit to this magnificent city.

First, it's vital to comprehend Siena's history. The city was created in the 12th century and was one of the major cities in Italy during the Middle Ages. Siena played a vital part in the trade of wool, silk, and spices, which contributed to creating its wealth and importance. Siena's rich history is reflected in its well-preserved medieval architecture, which includes tiny cobblestone alleys, gorgeous squares, and majestic palaces.

One of the most prominent structures in Siena is the Cathedral of Santa Maria Assunta, generally known as the Siena Cathedral. This remarkable Gothic building was created between 1215 and 1263 and is notable for its gorgeous inlaid marble floor and elaborate exterior. The cathedral is also home to numerous famous works of art, including a beautiful pulpit by Giovanni Pisano and other masterpieces by Michelangelo.

Another must-visit monument in Siena is the Piazza del Campo, a magnificent plaza that is regarded as one of the most beautiful in Italy. The square is the site of the Palio di Siena, a horse race that takes place twice a year and is a significant aspect of Siena's history and culture. The square is also home to various historic buildings, including the Palazzo Pubblico, the town hall of Siena, and the Torre del Mangia, a tall tower that offers beautiful views of the city.

Siena is particularly famed for its art, and there are various museums and galleries in the city that are worth seeing. The Pinacoteca Nazionale di Siena is one of the most prominent art museums in Italy and is home to an extensive collection of medieval and Renaissance art. The museum is housed in the Palazzo Dei Papi and exhibits works by many great artists, including Duccio di Buoninsegna, Simone Martini, and Ambrogio Lorenzetti.

In addition to its art and architecture, Siena is also recognized for its food and wine. The city is surrounded by the rolling hills of Tuscany, including Chianti we discussed before, and Brunello di Montalcino. There are various wine shops in Siena that offer tastings and excursions, allowing you to try some of the finest wines from the region.

Siena is also home to a strong food culture, and there are many restaurants and cafes in the city that serve classic Tuscan foods.

It is also notable for its many festivals and events, which are hosted throughout the year. One of the most famous events is the Palio di Siena, a horse race that takes place in the Piazza del Campo twice a year and is a major aspect of Siena's history and culture. The festival is a bright and spectacular display of pageantry, with elaborately costumed horses and riders representing different neighborhoods in the city.

Another prominent celebration in Siena is the Festa Della Madonna dell'Udienza, which is celebrated in June and honors the city's patron saint, the Madonna dell'Udienza. The celebration comprises a procession through the streets of Siena, accompanied by music and dance.

If you're a fan of shopping, you'll also enjoy exploring Siena's various shops and boutiques. The city is known for its high-quality leather items, and there are several establishments that specialize in leather shoes, belts, and purses. There are also many shops that sell traditional Tuscan pottery and ceramics, making it simple to purchase unique and lovely souvenirs to take back home.

Finally, for those who appreciate the great outdoors, Siena is a terrific site to explore the surrounding countryside. The city is surrounded by the rolling hills of Tuscany, which offer many options for hiking, cycling, and equestrian riding. Whether you're searching for a leisurely stroll or a more demanding excursion, the Tuscan countryside is a beautiful and serene respite from the rush and bustle of the city.

Siena is a city that genuinely has something for everyone. From its rich history and breathtaking architecture to its bustling cuisine and wine culture, there are endless reasons to visit this beautiful city. Whether you're traveling single or with your family,

Siena is guaranteed to present you with a wonderful and authentic Tuscan experience that you'll never forget.

Val d'Orcia

Val d'Orcia is a breathtakingly beautiful valley in the southern district of Siena. The valley is surrounded by undulating hills too, vineyards, olive orchards, and attractive old towns, making it one of the most picturesque locations in Italy. Val d'Orcia is noted for its beautiful landscapes, rich history, and cultural legacy.

Val d'Orcia is located in the province of Siena and encompasses an area of roughly 120 square kilometers. The valley is bordered by the towering peaks of the Amiata and Cetona mountains and is filled with charming villages and hamlets that date back to the Middle Ages. One of the most famous villages in the region is Pienza, famed for its wonderfully preserved Renaissance architecture and spectacular views of the valley. Other popular villages are San Quirico d'Orcia, Castiglione d'Orcia and Radicofani.

The environment of Val d'Orcia is defined by its rolling hills, vineyards, and olive orchards, interspersed with cypress trees and farmhouses. This unique environment has been classified as a UNESCO World Heritage Site due to its remarkable beauty and cultural significance. The valley is also home to a variety of thermal springs and spas, making it a popular destination for visitors seeking relaxation and renewal.

Val d'Orcia is also noted for its rich history and cultural heritage. The territory has been populated since ancient times, and the Etruscan civilization left its stamp on the terrain in the shape of spectacular tombs and fortifications. The valley was also an important hub of medieval culture and business, with a number of towns and villages that sprang up around trade routes and pilgrimage destinations.

One of the most prominent cultural landmarks in Val d'Orcia is the monastery of Sant'Antimo, a majestic Romanesque church that is regarded as one of the finest specimens of this style of construction in Italy. The abbey was erected in the 8th century and is a famous site for pilgrims and tourists alike.

Food and wine are also important components of the cultural heritage of Val d'Orcia. The region is famed for its olive oil and wine, and visitors can experience local delights at local vineyards and trattorias.

For those who appreciate outdoor sports, Val d'Orcia offers a multitude of chances for hiking, cycling, and horse riding. The valley is crisscrossed with well-marked trails that lead through the undulating hills and vineyards, affording spectacular views of the surrounding landscape. In the winter, the neighboring mountains are popular for skiing and snowboarding.

Val d'Orcia is also home to a variety of medieval castles, fortifications, and watchtowers that offer a look into the region's rich history. Castello di Castiglione d'Orcia is one of the most famous of these structures and is perched on a hilltop with beautiful views of the valley below.

It is one of the most scenic and culturally rich regions in Italy and is a must-visit destination for everyone who loves history, culture, food, and wine, or simply breathtaking vistas. Whether you're searching for a quiet break or an action-packed adventure, Val d'Orcia has something for everyone.

Pisa

Pisa is a city noted for its iconic leaning landmark, the Tower of Pisa. The city is also noted for its rich history and culture, as well as its stunning architecture and breathtaking landscapes.

One of the most popular sights in Pisa is the Leaning Tower of Pisa, often known as the Tower of Pisa or simply the Campanile. The tower is located in the Square of Miracles alternatively known as Piazza Dei Miracoli, a lovely square surrounded by numerous historic buildings and monuments, including the cathedral, Tower of Pisa is one of the most recognizable icons of Italy. The tower was originally intended as a bell tower for the nearby cathedral, but due to its inadequate foundation, it began to lean to one side during construction. Despite efforts to straighten it, the lean has become one of the tower's most famous aspects. The Piazza Dei Miracoli square is a UNESCO World Heritage Site and is regarded as one of the most important architectural ensembles in Italy. Visitors can tour the area, take in the spectacular vistas, and learn about the history of the structures and monuments.

The Pisa Cathedral is another important feature of the city. The cathedral, commonly known as the Cathedral of Santa Maria Assunta (Cathedral of Pisa), is a spectacular example of Romanesque architecture and is considered one of the finest specimens of its sort in Italy. The cathedral is also home to several major works of art, including a stunning pulpit and an exquisite mosaic floor.

In addition to its architectural and cultural highlights, Pisa is also noted for its stunning gardens and parks. One of the most popular parks in the city is the Botanical Garden and Museum of Pisa, which is home to a vast range of exotic and native plants, as well as a gorgeous greenhouse and a significant collection of cacti and succulents.

Pisa is also a terrific location for food enthusiasts, with a large selection of classic Tuscan cuisine to enjoy here as well.

For those taking an interest in history and culture, Pisa is home to several museums and galleries, including the National Archaeological Museum of Pisa, which houses a collection of ancient artifacts and art, and the Museo dell'Opera del Duomo, which is committed to the art and history of the Pisa Cathedral.

Pisa is also an excellent destination for shopping, with a vast selection of boutiques, marketplaces, and shopping malls to visit. The city is recognized for its leather items, including shoes, handbags, and jackets, as well as its jewelry and other handmade crafts.

Pisa is a city with a rich history, culture, and architecture that is likely to attract tourists of all interests. From the iconic leaning tower and the picturesque Piazza Dei Miracoli to the tasty Tuscan cuisine and scenic gardens, Pisa is a must-visit location in Italy.

Lucca

Lucca is recognized for its well-preserved Renaissance-era city walls, picturesque streets, and gorgeous gardens. It is also a popular destination for tourists due to its rich history, gorgeous architecture, and cultural heritage.

One of the primary tourist attractions of Lucca is the city walls, which date back to the 16th century. The walls were built to protect the city from invaders, but today they serve as a beautiful park that is excellent for strolling and taking in the sights. The walls are about 4 kilometers long and contain various towers and gates that offer wonderful views of the city and the surrounding countryside.

Another renowned site in Lucca is the Piazza dell'Anfiteatro, which is located in the center of the city. This ancient Roman amphitheater was built in the 1st century AD and is one of the best-preserved examples of its sort in the world. The area is surrounded by gorgeous Renaissance-era buildings, and it is a favorite spot for locals and tourists alike to relax and have a drink or a meal.

The Cathedral of St. Martin is another must-visit site in Lucca. The cathedral is one of the most important religious buildings in the city and is recognized for its majestic Romanesque architecture and gorgeous murals. The cathedral was established in the 11th century and has undergone various modifications and expansions over the ages. It is also home to several major works of art, including a picture by the famed Italian artist, Fra Angelico.

For those interested in history and culture, a visit to the Palazzo Pfanner is a must. This gorgeous palace was erected in the 17th century and is now home to a museum that highlights the history of Lucca and the surrounding region. The museum features a collection of antiquities, paintings, and sculptures that provide an insight into the city's rich history and cultural legacy.

Lucca is particularly famed for its gorgeous gardens and parks, notably the Giardino Botanico, which is one of the greatest botanical gardens in Italy. The garden is home to a vast variety of plants and flowers, as well as various walking routes and stunning panoramas. Another renowned park in Lucca is the Parco Pinocchio, which is a beautiful park that is dedicated to the famous children's book character, Pinocchio.

This place is also a fantastic spot to enjoy the local cuisine. The city is famous for its exquisite Tuscan meals, like Panzanella, a salad prepared from stale bread, tomatoes, onions, and basil, and prosciutto, cheese, and the famous Lucchese wine.

In addition to its many historical and cultural treasures, Lucca is also noted for its lively atmosphere and festivals. One of the most prominent events in the city is the Lucca Summer Festival, which is held every year between June and August. During the festival, the city's ancient streets are packed with music, art, and cultural acts. Visitors can enjoy a range of concerts and events, ranging from classical music to rock and pop.

For individuals who prefer outdoor activities, Lucca is a terrific location. The city is bordered by rolling hills and gorgeous scenery, making it a perfect place for cycling, hiking, and horse riding. The hills surrounding Lucca are also home to various vineyards and olive orchards, allowing visitors the opportunity to enjoy the local food and wine.

Lucca is also a fantastic location for visiting the surrounding region. The city is located just some distance from Florence, Pisa, and Siena. Visitors can take day trips to these destinations to enjoy the finest of Tuscany and explore some of Italy's most famous buildings and attractions, but won't be able to cover most.

Lucca is a must-visit location for anybody who is interested in history, culture, and the arts. The city offers a unique blend of history, culture, and modern facilities, making it a great destination for both tourists and families. Whether you are interested in seeing the city's many historical monuments, taking in its magnificent gardens and parks, or simply soaking up its bustling atmosphere, Lucca is sure to deliver an amazing experience.

San Gimignano

San Gimignano is a picturesque medieval hilltop town, it is noted for its well-preserved towers that have endured the test of time, making it one of the most popular tourist sites in Tuscany. With its medieval buildings, gorgeous landscapes, and rich cultural legacy, San Gimignano is a must-visit destination for anybody visiting Tuscany.

The village is located on a hilltop in the province of Siena. Visitors can reach San Gimignano by automobile or by taking a train to the nearby town of Poggibonsi and then getting a bus to the town center.

Upon arrival, visitors are immediately captivated by the town's stunning medieval architecture, particularly its iconic towers. At its height, San Gimignano was home to over 70 towers, many of which were built by affluent families as a sign of their wealth and power. Today, only 14 of the towers survive, but they are still a spectacular sight, standing high above the town and affording excellent views of the surrounding landscape.

One of the greatest ways to experience the town is by walking through its tiny, meandering lanes, lined with historic stone buildings, little stores, and charming eateries. The town is also home to several old churches, including the Church of Sant'Agostino, which includes a stunning fresco cycle by Bartolo di Fredi.

Another renowned site in San Gimignano is the Piazza Della Cisterna, a picturesque square encircled by medieval houses and capped with a well in the center. The square is an excellent area to stop for a coffee or gelato, or simply to observe the splendor of the town's architecture.

For those interested in history and art, the Museo Civico di San Gimignano is a must-visit. The museum is based in the Palazzo Comunale and exhibits a collection of works by artists such as Taddeo di Bartolo and Bartolo di Fredi, as well as valuable historic objects and documents.

For food enthusiasts, San Gimignano is a gourmet heaven, offering a wide selection of local specialties, including the famous Vernaccia wine, wild boar, and cured meats. Visitors can experience these delicacies at one of the town's many restaurants, or they can attend a cooking lesson to learn how to make traditional Tuscan cuisine.

In the neighboring area, guests can take a scenic drive or go on a trek to see the stunning views of the rolling hills and vineyards. For those interested in wine, there are many wineries in the vicinity that provide tastings and excursions, including the famed Castello di Verrazzano.

Finally, for those searching for a unique shopping experience, San Gimignano is home to many artisanal workshops, where tourists can observe local craftsmen at work and purchase handcrafted goods such as ceramics, leather goods, and jewelry.

San Gimignano is a unique and fascinating place that provides something for everyone. From its well-preserved medieval buildings and breathtaking surroundings to its rich cultural legacy and superb local cuisine, San Gimignano is a must-visit destination for anybody visiting Tuscany.

Volterra

Volterra is another hilltop town, with its well-preserved Etruscan ruins, and medieval walls. Volterra is a renowned tourist destination for history lovers and those seeking a taste of old-world charm.

The history of Volterra extends back to the Etruscan era, as indicated by the numerous tombs and remains that have been discovered in the vicinity. During the medieval period, Volterra became an important center of power, with a robust defensive system that protected its population from assaults. The town's affluence at this time may be seen in the many spectacular palaces and churches that still survive today, including the Palazzo Dei Priori, which was the seat of government for the town's oligarchic republic.

One of the town's most recognized attractions is the Palazzo Pretorio, a majestic Renaissance edifice that was originally the house of the governor of Volterra. Today, it houses a museum displaying the town's rich history and art, featuring exhibitions on Etruscan and medieval art and antiquities.

Volterra is also famed for its alabaster workshops, which have been creating high-quality alabaster objects for over five centuries. Visitors can see artists at work in the workshops, see finished goods on display in the town's many shops, and learn about the history of alabaster manufacturing in Volterra.

Another must-see site in Volterra is the Roman Theatre, which was built during the first century BC and is one of the best-preserved Roman theaters in Italy. The theater was used for shows, gladiatorial competitions, and other public events, and now it is a popular site for travelers who are interested in ancient history.

For anyone interested in researching the town's medieval past, a visit to the Porta all'Arco is a must. This is one of the original entrances to the town's defense system and has been kept in its original shape, affording a look into the past.

The town is surrounded by rolling hills and countryside, making it a popular location for outdoor enthusiasts. Visitors can hike or cycle in the surrounding countryside, take beautiful drives to explore the area, or simply rest and enjoy the peace and quiet of the Tuscan countryside.

Numerous local eateries dishing up classic Tuscan cuisine created from fresh, locally-sourced ingredients. Some popular foods to try are Panzanella.

With its well-preserved Etruscan ruins, spectacular architecture, and beautiful scenery, this hilltop town is a true treasure of the region and a tribute to the ongoing beauty and charm of the Tuscan way of life.

Montepulciano

Also recognized for its wine production and gorgeous Renaissance architecture. The town is situated in the province of Siena and is surrounded by vineyards that produce the renowned Vino Nobile di Montepulciano. The wine has been manufactured since the 14th century and is considered one of the best red wines in Tuscany.

Visitors to Montepulciano will be captivated by the town's charm and beauty, with winding cobbled lanes, stately palaces, and well-preserved medieval and Renaissance architecture. One of the primary attractions to see is the Comune di Montepulciano, a beautiful town hall located in the main square, Piazza Grande. The area is also home to the Montepulciano Cathedral, which dates back to the 15th century and displays a stunning façade with Gothic and Renaissance elements.

Walking about the town, you will find many other lovely churches, such as the church of Sant'agostino, the church of Santa Maria Dei Servi, and the church of San Biagio. Montepulciano is also home to several Renaissance palaces, notably the Palazzo Tarugi and the Palazzo Avignonesi.

For wine aficionados, Montepulciano provides a variety of wine-tasting opportunities. You can visit some of the town's many wineries, including the Cantina Contucci, where you can try their Vino Nobile di Montepulciano, as well as other local wines. Some of the wineries also provide tours of their vineyards and cellars, allowing visitors to learn more about the wine-making process.

Visitors can also sample local cheeses, such as pecorino, a sharp sheep's milk cheese, and the delightful, creamy ricotta.

Montepulciano is also widely renowned for its hot baths, which have been used for their therapeutic powers since Roman times. The most famous thermal bath in Montepulciano is the Bagni San Filippo, which is located just outside the town and boasts lovely thermal pools and natural waterfalls.

Visitors visiting Montepulciano can discover a choice of accommodation options, from historic palaces converted into hotels to modest, family-run bed and breakfasts. There are also a number of apartments and holiday homes available for rent, providing tourists the option to experience the town like a resident.

Cortona

Cortona is noted for its breathtaking views, medieval buildings, and rich cultural legacy. The town is a major tourist destination and is largely recognized as one of the most attractive and well-preserved medieval towns in Italy.

One of the primary attractions of Cortona is its medieval town, which is enclosed by old walls and gives spectacular views of the surrounding landscape. The town is littered with historic buildings, including medieval churches, palaces, and monasteries, many of which have been magnificently preserved and offer a look into the town's rich history.

One of the most noteworthy landmarks in Cortona is the Piazza Della Repubblica, the town's principal square. This bustling area is encircled by historic structures and is home to a multitude of businesses, restaurants, and cafes. Visitors to the town will also find a variety of noteworthy museums and art galleries, including the Museo dell'Accademia Etrusca and the Museo Diocesano, which offer an insight into the town's rich cultural legacy.

For outdoor aficionados, Cortona is a terrific destination to explore. The village is bordered by rolling hills, vineyards, and olive orchards, and is home to a multitude of walking and hiking paths that offer wonderful views of the countryside. Visitors can also explore the countryside by bike or horseback, or simply relax in one of the town's many parks and gardens.

For those interested in history, Cortona has a rich and fascinating past. The town was formerly a prominent center of the Etruscan civilization, and relics of this ancient civilization can still be found in the surrounding area. The town was also an important center of medieval culture and art, and today it is home to a variety of ancient structures and monuments that offer an insight into its rich history.

Cortona is a visit for everyone interested in Italian history. Whether you are interested in studying the town's rich heritage or soaking up the breathtaking views.

These are just a few of the numerous renowned tourist destinations in Tuscany.

Top Cuisine to Try Out

Tourists visiting Tuscany can expect to sample a range of delectable foods such as:

Bistecca alla Fiorentina

Bistecca Alla Fiorentina is a T-bone steak dish that originated in Florence. It is a cornerstone of Tuscan cuisine and is highly regarded for its soft, juicy meat and peculiar flavor.

The steak is sliced from the loin of the Chianina breed of cattle, which is endemic to Tuscany. The Chianina breed is one of the largest and oldest cattle breeds in the world and is noted for its high-quality meat. The steak is usually cooked over hot coals and seasoned simply with salt and pepper, allowing the natural flavor of the meat to shine through.

To create the dish, the steak is seared on both sides until it is browned and then cooked to the appropriate degree of doneness. It is normally served rare or medium-rare, with the center of the steak still pink. This cooking process allows the steak to preserve its juicy flavor and soft texture.

The dish is generally served with a side of roasted or grilled vegetables and potatoes, and it is also common to have a simple tomato or arugula salad on the side. It is often appreciated with a full-bodied red wine, such as a Chianti or a Brunello di Montalcino.

When eating it, it is usual to cut the steak into thick slices and then enjoy each slice with a fork and knife. This is because the steak is typically too huge to be consumed in one bite, and slicing it allows for better dispersion of the juices and flavors.

It's a favorite meal for special occasions and celebrations in Tuscany. It is typically offered at weddings, birthdays, and other events and is considered a sign of Tuscan hospitality and generosity.

When dining out, it is necessary to be aware that Bistecca alla Fiorentina is not a cheap meal. The high expense of the steak is related to the cost of breeding

Chianina cattle, as well as the big size of the steak itself. However, many restaurants in Tuscany serve smaller quantities of the steak, making it more accessible for people who want to sample it.

It is a renowned dish in Tuscany, famed for its soft, juicy meat and peculiar flavor. Whether consumed during a particular event or simply as a treat, this meal is a must-try for anyone visiting Tuscany who is interested in sampling the local food.

Ribollita

Ribollita is a substantial soup that originated in Tuscany, it is cooked using a variety of vegetables and beans. It is a traditional meal that has been loved by Tuscans for generations and continues to be a mainstay of Tuscan cuisine.

Visitors in Tuscany can enjoy the native flavors by sampling dishes like Ribollita, which is frequently available in the region's restaurants and cafes.

It is often created with components such as cannellini beans, carrots, kale, potatoes, onions, celery, and bread. The veggies are first sautéed in olive oil and then boiled in a delicious broth made from chicken or vegetable stock. The beans are then added to the soup and cooked until they are soft. Finally, chunks of stale bread are added to the soup and allowed to soak up the broth, imparting a delicious, hearty texture to the dish.

One of the distinctive qualities of this soup is that it is usually cooked with leftovers and old bread, making it an economical and delectable way to use up food that might otherwise go to waste. This makes it a fantastic recipe for busy families or those trying to save money on their grocery expenditures.

When visiting Tuscany, you can try Ribollita in a typical trattoria, or family-owned restaurant. Most trattorias serve the soup as a main meal, generally accompanied by a basic green salad and a glass of local red wine. Wine is an integral part of the dining experience in Tuscany regions.

If you're interested in cooking Ribollita at home, you may find several recipes online or in cookbooks dedicated to Tuscan food. Some recipes call for utilizing specific ingredients like cavolo nero (black kale), which is a variety of kale that is widely used in Tuscan cooking. However, you may also use ordinary kale or other leafy greens like Swiss chard if you can't find cavolo nero in your local grocery shop.

When creating Ribollita at home, it's crucial to use good quality olive oil, as this is the key source of flavor in the meal. Additionally, use a delicious broth and make sure to let the soup simmer for at least an hour, enabling the flavors to develop and mingle together.

Ribollita is a fantastic dish for a winter day, as its substantial, warming flavors can warm you up from the inside out. It's also a terrific alternative for vegetarians and those following a plant-based diet, as it's packed with healthful components like beans and leafy greens.

Regardless of how you consume it, Ribollita is a tasty and nutritious dish that is likely to become a fixture in your home.

Pappa al Pomodoro

Pappa al Pomodoro is a typical Tuscan meal prepared from bread, tomatoes, olive oil, garlic, and basil. It is a warm and soothing soup that is a mainstay of Tuscan cuisine. This meal is generally served as a main course for lunch or supper, but it can also be eaten as a light snack or appetizer.

If you are visiting Tuscany and are interested in sampling Pappa al Pomodoro, you will find it on the menu of most classic Tuscan restaurants. Many local establishments pride themselves on delivering authentic and tasty Pappa al Pomodoro, cooked with the freshest and best quality ingredients. The meal is also typically featured on the menu in trattorias, osterias, and agriturismos, which are farm-to-table restaurants that specialize in local and seasonal cuisine.

When ordering Pappa al Pomodoro, you may expect to be served a bowl of rich tomato soup with chunks of bread floating in it. The bread is normally made from a dense, rustic loaf and is allowed to soak up the tomato liquid, giving it a rich and savory taste. The meal is generally seasoned with fresh basil and garlic, which give it a vibrant and herbaceous flavor. Olive oil is also a significant element in Pappa al Pomodoro, and many Tuscan restaurants will add high-quality extra-virgin olive oil to improve the flavor of the meal.

If you are staying in Tuscany for a longer period of time, you may also want to explore making Pappa al Pomodoro at home. This dish is really easy to create and can be prepared in just a few simple steps. To make Pappa al Pomodoro, you will need ripe tomatoes, garlic, basil, olive oil, and bread. Start by heating the olive oil in a large saucepan and adding the chopped garlic. Next, add the chopped tomatoes and basil to the pan and let the mixture simmer for several minutes. Finally, add the bread to the stew, allowing it to soak up the tomato broth. Serve hot and enjoy your delicious Pappa al Pomodoro.

When it comes to dining in Tuscany, it is vital to recognize that the local culture lays a high focus on the quality of ingredients and the preparation of food. Many Tuscan restaurants get their products from local farms and use traditional cooking methods to make wonderful genuine dishes.

When combined with a glass of Chianti, Pappa al Pomodoro makes for a superb supper that truly represents the flavors and traditions of Tuscan cuisine.

Crostini

One of the most popular local delicacies in Tuscany is crostini, which are small, toasted slices of bread topped with a variety of fillings.

It can be found in many forms across Tuscany and is a mainstay of Tuscan cuisine. They are commonly served as an appetizer or a snack and may be found in local cafés, trattorias, and markets. The typical preparation for crostini involves toasting slices of crusty bread, rubbing them with garlic, then topping them with a mixture of items such as olive oil, cheese, or cured meats.

One of the most famous versions of crostini in Tuscany is Crostini Alla Toscana, which has toppings such as chicken liver pâté, mushrooms, and truffles. Another famous variety is crostini di Fegatini, which is cooked with chicken liver and capers. For those who prefer a sweeter choice, crostini with Nutella or honey, and ricotta cheese is also popular.

Crostini can be combined with a range of local wines, such as Chianti or Brunello di Montalcino, which are produced in the neighboring hills of Tuscany. In addition to being a delightful snack or appetizer, crostini is also a versatile dish that can be readily altered to fit various tastes and preferences.

Porchetta

Porchetta is a traditional Italian meal known to be a savory and delectable roasted pig that is seasoned with garlic, rosemary, and fennel, then rolled, knotted, and slow-roasted until tender and moist. The outcome is a delicious pork roast with crispy crackling on the surface and juicy flesh on the inside.

Visitors can find porchetta prepared in numerous forms, from sandwiches and street cuisine to luxury restaurant entrees. The best way to sample Tuscany's porchetta is to attend a local market or food festival, where vendors offer out hot, juicy slices of the roast on crusty bread, topped with salsa verde or other traditional condiments.

When it comes to creating porchetta, the trick is to start with high-quality ingredients, like a delicious pork belly, fresh herbs, and extra virgin olive oil. The meat is first marinated overnight in a blend of herbs and spices, then rolled and knotted with string to keep it together during cooking. After that, it is roasted in a moderate oven for several hours, until the skin is crispy and the meat is moist and soft.

One of the best sites to taste porchetta in Tuscany is the town of Arezzo, where the local delicacy is called "porchetta di Ariccia." This town is famed for its wonderful porchetta, which is produced from free-range pigs bred on local farms. The meat is seasoned with garlic, rosemary, and fennel then roasted for many hours until crispy and golden brown. Visitors can find porchetta served in local pubs and restaurants, and it is also offered at local food markets and festivals.

Another fantastic destination for porchetta aficionados is the town of Florence, where visitors can get a range of delicious pig meals, including porchetta. In Florence, the porchetta is often served as a sandwich, with juicy slices of pork nestled between pieces of crusty bread and topped with salsa verde or other condiments. This is a fantastic dish to take on the go while touring the city or to enjoy as a light lunch or snack.

For those who want a more formal dining experience, there are also several gourmet restaurants in Tuscany that serve porchetta as a main dish. At these establishments, the porchetta is commonly coupled with sides such as roasted vegetables, mashed potatoes, or a simple salad, making it a full and well-rounded meal.

Visitors can also sample porchetta in a new way by attending a local food festival, where sellers set up stalls to offer up hot slices of pig and other tasty specialties. These festivals are a terrific opportunity to sample a range of local cuisine and explore the region's culinary heritage. Some of the most popular food festivals in Tuscany are the "Sagra del Maiale" in the town of Castellina Marittima, and the "Festa del Porchetta" in the town of San Giovanni Valdarno.

Porchetta is a must-try meal for anybody visiting the region. Whether served as a sandwich, a main dish at a gourmet restaurant, or as part of a food festival, this savory roast pig is a wonderful and authentic taste of Tuscany's culinary heritage. So, whether you're a foodie or just seeking for a pleasant lunch, make sure to sample porchetta on your next vacation to Tuscany.

Cantucci

Cantucci are crunchy, almond-based biscuits that originated in the Tuscan city of Prato in the 19th century. They were typically created with simple components such as almonds, wheat, sugar, and eggs. Today, Cantucci comes in numerous flavors including chocolate, pistachio, and hazelnut.

To make Cantucci, the dough is made into a log, baked, and then sliced into individual biscuits. The biscuits are then baked a second time to make them crispy and dry. This double-baking technique is what gives Cantucci their particular crunch, making them suitable for dipping in a sweet dessert wine such as Vin Santo.

Cantucci are generally eaten with a sweet wine called Vin Santo, which is made from Trebbiano or Malvasia grapes. Vin Santo is a dessert wine that is sweet and nutty, making it the perfect complement to Cantucci's almond flavor. To drink Cantucci and Vin Santo like a true Tuscan, dip a biscuit into the wine and relish the mix of crispy biscuit and sweet wine.

It is simple to find Cantucci and Vin Santo in wine shops and cafes around the region. However, the greatest place to try Cantucci is in the city of Prato, where they originated. In Prato, you may visit traditional bakeries and eat freshly made Cantucci with a glass of Vin Santo.

Cantucci, also known as biscotti di Prato, is a must-try treat in Tuscany. They are crunchy, almond-based biscuits that are traditionally eaten with Vin Santo, a sweet dessert wine.

Schiacciata alla Fiorentina

Tuscany Schiacciata Alla Fiorentina is a classic dish that originated in Florence. The dish is a form of thin-crust pizza, and its name directly translates to "Florentine-style flattened bread."

Schiacciata alla Fiorentina is a sort of flatbread that is produced with a simple dough that consists of water, flour, yeast, salt, and olive oil. The dough is then covered with olive oil, salt, and rosemary, and baked until crispy. This pizza is generally served as an appetizer or a light snack and is often eaten with a glass of red wine.

Schiacciata alla Fiorentina is produced with the same dough as the famous Tuscan bread, which is known for its simplicity and lack of sugar, butter, and other ingredients. The crust is thin and crispy, with a somewhat chewy texture. The olive oil used in the dough and on top of the pizza gives it a particular, rich flavor that is characteristic of Tuscan cuisine.

One of the best venues to try Schiacciata alla Fiorentina is in Florence itself. The city is rich with classic pizzerias that have been cooking this meal for centuries, utilizing the same techniques and ingredients passed down from their forefathers. Some of the most popular pizzerias in Florence are Il Teatro del Sale, Il Pizzaiuolo, and La Bottega del Buon Caffè.

Visitors to Florence can also take cooking workshops where they can learn how to create Schiacciata alla Fiorentina and other classic Tuscan meals. These lessons are a terrific opportunity to learn about the local cuisine and culture and to get a flavor of Tuscany in a hands-on way.

In addition to traditional pizzerias and cooking schools, Schiacciata alla Fiorentina may also be found in many cafés, pubs, and restaurants throughout Tuscany. Visitors can eat this delicacy while enjoying the magnificent vistas of the rolling hills, olive trees, and vineyards that are characteristic of this region.

Chianti, Brunello di Montalcino, and Vino Nobile di Montepulciano, these wines are the perfect match for Schiacciata alla Fiorentina.

Schiacciata alla Fiorentina is a delectable meal that is a must-try for everyone visiting the region. With its thin, crunchy crust, deep olive oil flavor, and simple toppings, this meal is a true taste of Tuscany. Whether served in a traditional pizza, a cafe, or at home after taking a culinary class, Schiacciata alla Fiorentina is a meal that is guaranteed to be remembered long after the trip is done.

Gelato

For those wishing to indulge in a sweet treat during their vacation, Tuscany is home to some of the best gelatos in the world. Let's examine the history of gelato in Tuscany, the typical flavors, and some of the best venues to try it.

Gelato is a frozen treat that originated in Italy and is comparable to ice cream. The difference between the two is that gelato is produced with more milk and less cream, resulting in a richer and creamier texture. It is also churned at a slower speed, which creates less air and results in a denser and smoother texture. Gelato has been a staple in Italy for centuries and is considered a work of art by Italian gelato makers.

In Tuscany, gelato has a lengthy history, with the earliest known gelato store established in Florence in the 16th century. The gelato was produced with simple materials, such as milk, sugar, and fruit, and was relished by the wealthy and the poor alike. Over the years, the popularity of gelato has only grown, and it has become a mainstay of Italian culture.

When it comes to classic flavors in Tuscany, there is a handful that stands out. One of the most popular is stracciatella, a taste formed with chocolate shavings and a creamy foundation. Another popular flavor is Nocciola, produced with hazelnuts, which are farmed in the region. In Tuscany, gelato is also produced with local ingredients, such as honey, lemon, and lavender, giving it a unique and distinct taste.

One of the best spots to try gelato in Tuscany is Florence. The city is home to some of the top gelato businesses in the region, including Gelateria La Carraia and Il Gelato di Filo. Both of these shops provide a wide assortment of tastes and use only the freshest and highest-quality ingredients. In addition to typical flavors, these establishments also provide unique and inventive flavors, such as balsamic vinegar and olive oil.

Another fantastic place to try gelato in Tuscany is Pisa. The city is home to a variety of gelato establishments, notably Gelateria de' Coltelli and Gelateria Di Toto. These establishments offer a selection of flavors, including conventional and innovative, and employ only the freshest ingredients.

If you're searching for a more classic gelato experience, then a visit to Siena is a must. The city is noted for its gelato stores, including Gelateria Dondoli and Gelateria pasticceria la bottega del Castello. Both of these shops provide a choice of traditional and innovative flavors, utilizing only the freshest and highest-quality ingredients.

From traditional flavors, such as stracciatella and nocciola, to unusual and inventive ones, such as balsamic vinegar and olive oil, there is something for everyone in Tuscany's gelato stores. Whether you're a gelato enthusiast or a beginner to the world of frozen treats, a vacation to Tuscany is not complete without trying its famed gelato.

Chianti wine

Chianti is a sort of wine that derives from the Chianti region. This area has been producing wine for generations. Chianti wine is derived from the Sangiovese grape, which is noted for its bright and fruity characteristics, and it is regarded one of the most popular red wines in the world.

Visitors to Tuscany can take part in a wine-tasting tour of the Chianti region, which normally includes stops at numerous local vineyards. These trips offer an opportunity to learn about the wine-making process, taste several types of Chianti wine, and meet the local winemakers who are passionate about their work.

One of the most popular wineries to visit is the Castello di Ama, which is located in the heart of the Chianti Classico district. This winery has been making wine since the 14th century, and it offers tastings and tours of its cellars and vineyards. Visitors can also enjoy a meal at the winery's restaurant, which includes traditional Tuscan meals coupled with the estate's wines.

Another notable winery is the Tenuta di Arceno, which is located in the southern section of the Chianti region. This winery specializes in making high-quality Chianti wine and also gives tastings and tours to guests. Tenuta di Arceno also has a wonderful view of the surrounding hills, which makes it a popular site to stop at for a picnic.

Finally, for those who want to take home a taste of the Chianti region, local shops, and marketplaces sell a range of Chianti wine, as well as other local items, such as olive oil, cheese, and cured meats. Visitors can also purchase wine online or at local wine shops, which frequently have a broad range of Chianti wine from different producers.

Chianti region is a must-visit location for anyone who loves wine, history, and picturesque scenery. The Chianti region offers guests a true sense of Tuscany, and it is likely to be a memorable encounter

Fagioli all'uccelletto

Fagioli all'uccelletto is a typical Italian dish made with cannellini beans and tomato sauce. It is often served with slices of toasted bread that have been smeared with garlic. The meal is titled "all'uccelletto" which means "small bird-style," probably because the beans and sauce resemble a bird's nest and the bread resembles bird eggs.

This dish is traditionally regarded as a rustic and comfortable dinner, often eaten as a main course in Tuscany, Italy. It is produced by cooking cannellini beans in a tomato-based sauce seasoned with garlic, rosemary, and sage until the flavors have melted together. The toasted bread is then placed on top of the beans and sauce, and the dish is finished with a sprinkle of olive oil.

It is a popular meal among tourists visiting Tuscany, as it is a traditional food that is characteristic of the region's cuisine. It is widely offered at local trattorias and osterias and is also a staple dish in home cooking.

It is a simple yet tasty dish cooked with cannellini beans, tomato sauce, garlic, and herbs, served over toasted bread. It is a popular dish among tourists visiting Tuscany and is a mainstay of the region's cuisine.

Pappardelle

Pappardelle is a type of pasta that hails from Tuscany, a region in central Italy. The pasta is created from a simple dough of egg, flour, and salt, and is often wider and flatter than other forms of pasta. The most typical method to serve Pappardelle is with a heavy meat-based sauce, such as a ragù, however, it can also be served with lighter sauces made with fresh ingredients, like tomato and basil.

In Tuscany, Pappardelle is considered a staple cuisine and is often served in restaurants and homes alike. Many traditional Tuscan recipes have been passed down from generation to generation, giving the dish a rich cultural heritage.

Visitors to Tuscany can experience Pappardelle in a number of ways, such as attending culinary workshops where they can learn to create pasta from scratch and sample it with different sauces. Additionally, many local restaurants feature Pappardelle on their menu and it is also feasible to purchase pre-made pasta from local markets or specialty food stores.

Pappardelle is a wonderful and adaptable meal that is a vital element of Tuscany's cuisine culture. Whether you're a foodie or just seeking for a tasty lunch, sampling Pappardelle in Tuscany is a must for any traveler visiting the region.

Risotto alla Milanese

Risotto alla Milanese is a typical meal from Milan, which is produced by cooking arborio rice in a blend of broth and wine, then completed with additions such as saffron and Parmesan cheese. Although it is a dish from Milan, it may also be savored in Tuscany, a region in central Italy famed for its rich culinary tradition.

Tourists visiting Tuscany can try it at numerous local restaurants and trattorias that provide Italian food. This meal is frequently served as a first course, although it can also be a main dish if given in a bigger size. Its creamy texture, rich flavor, and delicate aroma of saffron make it a popular option among guests.

Traditional Risotto alla Milanese in Tuscany regions is frequently produced with the same ingredients and procedures as in Milan, but local chefs may add their own touches or changes to the meal. Some may use different types of broth or wine or add local ingredients such as mushrooms or truffles to enhance the flavor.

Overall, Risotto alla Milanese is a delightful and classic Italian meal that is definitely worth eating during a vacation to Tuscany. Whether served as a first course or a main dish, it is sure to be a memorable culinary experience for tourists and locals alike.

Tagliatelle al tartufo

Tagliatelle al Tartufo is a typical Tuscan dish prepared with egg tagliatelle pasta and truffles. The meal is often served as a main course and is renowned for its rich, earthy flavor.

Truffles, the major ingredient of the meal, are edible fungi found in the woodlands of Tuscany. They are widely sought after for their peculiar, musky flavor and are typically used as a condiment for pasta and other foods. In Tagliatelle al Tartufo, tiny shavings of fresh truffle are added to a simple sauce cooked with butter, Parmesan cheese, and freshly ground black pepper. The sauce is then combined with freshly produced tagliatelle pasta to create a dinner that is both tasty and elegant.

Tagliatelle al Tartufo is typically served in expensive restaurants in Tuscany and is a popular dish among tourists visiting the region. The dish is generally accompanied by a glass of full-bodied red wine, such as Chianti Classico, which helps to balance the rich tastes of the truffle and Parmesan.

It is a must-try for anybody visiting Tuscany who likes pasta and wants to experience the unique flavors of the region. Whether you are a foodie, a gourmet, or simply adore delicious Italian cuisine, this dish is sure to satisfy your demands and make a lasting impression.

Torta della Nonna

Torta della Nonna, commonly known as "Grandmother's Cake," is a traditional Tuscan dessert that is made composed of a sweet shortcrust pastry base, filled with a creamy custard made with eggs, sugar, lemon zest and vanilla, and topped with pine nuts. It is normally served in slices, sprinkled with powdered sugar.

The dish is supposed to have originated in the hills of Tuscany and was a staple in the homes of Italian grandmothers. It is currently a popular dish found in many Tuscan pastry shops and restaurants and is a must-try for anyone visiting the region.

Torta della Nonna is a famous example of simple and comfortable Italian cuisine, utilizing only a few ingredients to make a tasty and gratifying dessert. It's great to end a meal with and is commonly paired with a cup of espresso or a glass of Vin Santo, a sweet dessert wine usually brewed in Tuscany.

Be sure to try Torta della Nonna at a local pastry store or restaurant and have a taste of authentic Tuscan culinary heritage.

Castagnaccio

Castagnaccio is a typical Tuscan cake prepared from chestnut flour, olive oil, salt, and water. It's a rustic dessert that's commonly served in fall when chestnuts are in season. Castagnaccio is commonly flavored with rosemary and raisins, and sometimes with pine nuts or fennel seeds.

Tourists visiting Tuscany can sample Castagnaccio at local bakeries, restaurants, and marketplaces. Some of the greatest spots to enjoy Castagnaccio in Tuscany include the towns of Florence, Pisa, and Siena, where the dessert is a mainstay in local cuisine. Visitors can also join culinary workshops and cuisine tours that demonstrate the traditional dishes of Tuscany, like Castagnaccio.

In addition to its excellent flavor, Castagnaccio is also noted for its simplicity and versatility. It may be eaten as a dessert or as a snack, and it's a fantastic alternative for vegetarians and individuals with gluten sensitivities since it's prepared with chestnut flour and doesn't include wheat. Overall, Castagnaccio is a must-try for anyone visiting Tuscany who wishes to taste the region's traditional cuisine culture.

Acquacotta

Acquacotta is a traditional Tuscan soup made from simple and affordable ingredients such as bread, vegetables, and eggs. It was originally intended as a supper for rural workers and has since become a staple dish in Tuscan cuisine.

The soup is produced by cooking bread, tomato, onion, garlic, and olive oil together until the bread softens and the ingredients form a thick broth. Eggs are then added to the soup, which is poached in the broth and served as a topping.

Visitors to Tuscany can enjoy Acquacotta at numerous local restaurants, which typically promote it as a seasonal or daily special. Some restaurants also serve versions of the soup, utilizing various ingredients or combining local spices and flavors.

In addition to its exquisite taste, Acquacotta is particularly treasured for its cultural significance as a typical Tuscan dish. It is a simple and comfortable dish that speaks to the region's history and heritage, making it a popular choice for tourists wanting a real flavor of Tuscany.

Cacciucco

Cacciucco is a classic fish stew that originates from the coastal districts of Tuscany. It is created with a variety of different types of fish, onions, tomatoes, garlic, white wine, and chili pepper, cooked together in a tasty broth. It is generally served with toasted bread that has been rubbed with garlic and drizzled with olive oil, known as "crostini."

In Tuscany, Cacciucco is a favorite dish for celebrating special occasions and is commonly enjoyed as a family supper. It is also a popular dish for tourists to enjoy when visiting Tuscany, as it is considered a taste of the region's traditional cuisine.

There are several versions of Cacciucco, and each family or restaurant may have their own distinctive recipe. However, the meal keeps loyal to its beginnings with its use of fresh, locally-sourced ingredients and its concentration on robust, aromatic components.

Cacciucco is a must-try meal for anybody visiting Tuscany and wishing to taste the region's rich culinary tradition. Whether enjoyed at a family meal or at a local restaurant, this dish is sure to be a memorable and delightful experience.

You must have noticed, that with some of the meals listed wine is best consumed with them, it's because wine is an important part of Tuscan cuisine. Tuscany provides a range of delectable foods that are produced utilizing fresh, local ingredients.

Best time to visit Tuscany

The best time to visit Tuscany depends on numerous aspects, including weather, crowds, and the type of activities you plan to partake in.

Spring (March to May) is a popular time to visit Tuscany as the weather is moderate and the landscape is awash with bright blooms. The renowned hills of Tuscany turn green and the famous vineyards come to life. This season is perfect for outdoor activities, such as hiking and bicycling, as well as visiting the many lovely gardens and parks in the region. Additionally, the crowds are not as thick during this time of year, allowing you to enjoy Tuscany's beauty and charm at a more relaxed pace.

Summer (June to August) is considered the high season in Tuscany, with warm and sunny weather that attracts travelers from all over the world. This season is great for beachgoers many outdoor festivals and activities take place during the summer months, making it an exciting time to visit Tuscany. However, be prepared for crowds and hefty prices, especially in famous tourist spots.

Fall (September to November) is another fantastic time to visit Tuscany as the weather remains mild and the people begin to thin out. The fall season is exceptionally gorgeous in Tuscany as the hills turn golden with the changing foliage and the vineyards are harvested. This is a wonderful time for food and wine enthusiasts to visit Tuscany, as the region is recognized for its delicious cuisine and superb wine. Additionally, the fall months are a perfect time to visit the many historic towns and cities in the region, such as Florence, Pisa, and Siena.

Winter (December to February) is the low season in Tuscany, with pleasant temperatures and fewer tourists. This is a quieter and more pleasant season to visit Tuscany, and the lack of crowds makes it simpler to explore the region's many historical and cultural monuments. Additionally, several of the region's major art museums, such as the Uffizi Gallery in Florence, are less crowded during the winter months.

Regardless of the time of year you visit Tuscany, there are many must-see attractions and activities that should not be missed.

Beaches in Tuscany

Some of the most popular beaches here include Marina di Pisa, Marina di Grosseto, and Castiglione della Pescaia. Marina di Pisa is a long, sandy beach that is located near the city of Pisa. This beach is great for families with children because it is reasonably shallow and offers calm waves. There are also several restaurants, cafes, and ice cream stores nearby, so you can enjoy a nice dinner or a refreshing snack as you relax on the beach.

Marina di Grosseto is another popular beach, and it is recognized for its beautiful, white sand and crystal-clear seas. This beach is also perfect for families with children, as it is highly safe and has a shallow entry into the water. There are also plenty of restaurants and cafés around, so you can have a wonderful meal or a cool drink while you soak up the sun.

Castiglione della Pescaia is a lovely, ancient town located on the coast of Tuscany. This town is noted for its stunning beaches, which are bordered by lush green hills and crystal-clear waters. The major beach in Castiglione della Pescaia is called the Spiaggia Lunga, and it is a long, sandy beach that is great for swimming, sunbathing, and relaxing. There are also several restaurants and cafés in the town, so you can enjoy a nice meal or a refreshing drink as you explore the surrounding region.

Another popular beach is Cala Violina, which is located in the province of Grosseto. This beach is considered one of the most beautiful beaches in Italy, and it is famous for its crystal-clear seas and fine, white sand. The name of the beach, Cala Violina, means "violin cove" in Italian, and it is said that the sound of the waves breaking on the shore sounds like a violin being played.

In addition to these prominent beaches, there are many additional beaches in Tuscany that are worth seeing. For example, there is the beach in Viareggio, which is known for its famed Carnival and its long, sandy beach that is great for swimming and sunbathing. There is also the beach at Forte dei Marmi, which is a trendy and chic beach town that is popular with the wealthy and famous.

When visiting the beaches in Tuscany, it is necessary to be careful of the environment and to take care of the natural beauty of this region. For example, it is crucial to use approved garbage cans and not litter on the beach, as this can disrupt the sensitive ecosystems that occur along the coast.

Whether you are a family with children, a group of friends, or a solitary traveler, you are sure to have a wonderful experience in this amazing region. So, pack your sunscreen, bring your beach towel, and get ready to experience the

Traveling Essentials

Packing for a Tuscany holiday might be a bit intimidating, but good planning is vital to make the most of your trip. Whether you are traveling by plane or by vehicle, packing the appropriate stuff can make all the difference in the world.

General Essentials

Attire: Tuscany is famed for its warm and sunny weather, so light and airy clothing is a requirement. Pack cotton or linen shirts, shorts, skirts, and dresses, as well as a light sweater or jacket for chilly evenings. Remember to pack good shoes for walking, as Tuscany is filled with gorgeous scenery and old cities to explore.

Sun Protection: The sun in Tuscany may be fierce, so carry a wide-brimmed hat, sunglasses, and sunblock. A parasol or umbrella can also be a valuable device for giving shade during your travels.

Amenities: Don't forget your basic toiletries, such as toothbrush and toothpaste, shampoo, and soap. Pack travel-sized products to save room and carry a first-aid kit, containing painkillers, band-aids, and any prescription prescriptions you may need.

Camera: Tuscany is rich in the magnificent scenery and historic sites, so a camera is a must. If you're an avid photographer, consider taking a high-end camera or accessories, such as a tripod or additional batteries. If you're not a photography aficionado, a smartphone camera is still a terrific method to document your moments.

Cash and Credit Cards: Make sure to include some local currency, such as the Euro, as well as credit cards for larger transactions. Be mindful of any international transaction costs your credit card may incur and consider getting a travel-specific credit card with no foreign transaction fees.

Travel Documents: Don't forget your passport, trip visa (if required), and any crucial travel documents, such as your hotel reservation or tour itinerary.

Portable Charger: With all the traveling and photo-taking you'll be doing, your electronic gadgets may run low on battery. Pack a portable charger to keep your phone and camera charged and ready for usage.

Travel Adaptor: Tuscany utilizes a sort of plug that is different from many other countries, so make sure to carry a travel adapter to keep your electronics charged.

Snacks and Water Bottles: Tuscany is famed for its great food and wine, but it can be pricey to eat out for every meal. Pack food, such as trail mix or granola bars, and bring a reusable water bottle to save money and avoid trash.

Travel Cushion: If you're going to Tuscany, consider carrying a travel pillow to guarantee a comfortable flight.

You may also want to carry a book or magazine to enjoy during downtime, and a map or GPS gadget to assist you find your route, although we think your mobile device Map will suffice as it works on the go.

With careful preparation and packing, you can ensure that your trip is as memorable and pleasurable as possible.

Hiking Essentials

If you're planning a hiking holiday, it's crucial to be prepared and carry the correct gear to make the most of your experience. Here is a detailed list of stuff you should consider packing for a comfortable and pleasurable hiking in Tuscany.

Backpack: A solid quality backpack is a must-have for every hiking expedition. Choose a backpack that is roomy enough to hold all your belongings and is comfortable to use for extended durations. Make sure it has comfortable straps, a strong structure, and adequate pockets for organizing.

Footwear: Good hiking shoes are a necessary for Tuscany's rocky terrain. Look for shoes with a supportive, comfortable fit, and a firm grip for uneven surfaces. You can also pick waterproof shoes to keep your feet dry in case of rain.

Clothes: Pack clothing that is suited for the weather and the level of physical activity. Tuscany may be warm in the summer and cool in the spring and fall, so prepare appropriately. Avoid cotton, as it can take a long time to dry. Choose quick-drying and breathable fabrics like polyester, nylon, and merino wool.

Hydration: It's crucial to stay hydrated while trekking in Tuscany, so bring plenty of water. A hydration pack, water bottles, or a hydration bladder are all good solutions. Also, consider packing water purification tablets in case you come across a stream or river.

Food and Snacks: Pack enough food and snacks to nourish your body for the duration of your hike. Energy bars, trail mix, fruit, and sandwiches are all wonderful options. Don't forget to bring a small cooler or insulated lunch bag to keep your food fresh.

Navigation Equipment: Tuscany might have poorly designated trails, so it's necessary to have navigation tools to assist you stay on course. A map and compass are must-haves, but a GPS device can also be useful. Make careful to get offline maps and plan your journey before you depart.

First Aid Bag: Accidents can happen while hiking, so it's crucial to pack a well-stocked first aid kit. Your kit should include bandages, gauze, adhesive tape, antiseptic wipes, pain medicines, and any other important materials you may need in case of an emergency.

Headlamp or Flashlight: Tuscany's paths can be poorly lit, and the sun sets early in the fall and winter months. Pack a headlamp or flashlight with fresh batteries to help you navigate in the dark.

Sun Protection: Tuscany's bright weather may be strong, especially during the summer months. Pack a hat, sunglasses, and sunblock to protect your skin from damaging UV rays.

Rain Gear: Tuscany can experience sudden rain showers, so it's vital to pack rain gear to keep yourself dry. A waterproof jacket, leggings, and pack cover are all must-haves for any hiking excursion in Tuscany.

Extra Clothes: Tuscany's weather can vary quickly, so it's a good idea to carry extra layers to be warm and comfortable. A fleece jacket, down vest, or an extra shirt are all wonderful possibilities.

Trash Bag: Help keep Tuscany's trails clean by packing a little trash bag to carry off any debris you make.

Packing the correct gear for your Tuscany hiking vacation is vital for a safe and happy experience. Make sure to take a decent quality backpack, suitable boots, adequate clothing, enough food and water, navigation equipment, a first aid kit, headlamp or flashlight.

Swimming Essentials

If your objective or part of your goal is to spend time swimming in the many pools and lakes in the region. To make the procedure a bit easier, here is a thorough list of stuff that you should consider bringing for a Tuscany swimming trip.

Swimwear: Pack at least 2-3 swimsuits or trunks, as well as a number of cover-ups or t-shirts to wear over your swimwear.

Sun Protection: The Tuscany region is known for its warm weather, so make sure you take plenty of sunscreen with a high SPF rating, as well as a hat or visor to protect your face and eyes from the sun. A good pair of sunglasses is also crucial.

Beach Towels: Pack a couple of towels for usage both in and out of the water. Lightweight, quick-drying towels are excellent, as they are easy to pack and will not take up too much space in your luggage.

Water Shoes: Consider taking a pair of water shoes if you plan on swimming in lakes or rivers, as these can protect your feet from sharp rocks and other hazards that can be in the water.

Pool or Beach Toys: If you have children or just want to have some fun in the water, try taking a few pool or beach toys such as inflatable rafts, beach balls, or frisbees.

Snorkeling Gear: If you plan on snorkeling or exploring underwater in Tuscany, make sure to carry a snorkel, mask, and fins.

Dry Bag: If you plan on spending a lot of time near the water, a dry bag can be quite beneficial for keeping your possessions safe and dry.

Flip Flops: Pack a pair of flip-flops for usage around the pool or on the beach. They are easy to put on and off and are considerably more comfortable than going around with bare feet.

Swim Caps: If you have long hair, consider bringing a swim cap to keep it out of your face while swimming.

Personal Hygiene Goods: Don't forget to bring basic personal hygiene items such as a toothbrush and toothpaste, shampoo and conditioner, and any other amenities you may require.

In addition to the materials indicated above, it is also a good idea to carry a few extra items to make your Tuscany swimming trip more comfortable and pleasurable.

Lightweight Clothing: Pack lightweight clothing that is comfortable and simple to wear in the heat. Breathable, cotton, or linen materials are suitable.

Sun Hat or Umbrella: If you plan on spending a lot of time in the sun, a sun hat or umbrella can be a lifesaver. They will give much-needed shade and protect you from the sun's damaging rays.

Portable Cooler: If you plan on spending a lot of time near the water, a portable cooler can be very beneficial. Fill it with drinks and snacks, and you will have everything you need for a day of relaxation by the pool or on the beach.

Beach Chair or Lounge Chair: A beach chair or lounge chair is essential for anyone who wishes to spend a lot of time by the ocean. They are comfy, convenient to transport, and may be adjusted to your personal level of comfort.

Camera: Don't forget to pack a camera to capture all of the great moments you will make during your Tuscany holiday.

When packing for a Tuscany swimming holiday, the goal is to prioritize comfort, ease, and pragmatism. Make sure you take products that will shield you from the sun, as well as stuff that will make your time by the water more enjoyable.

Traveling Itinerary

Here is a suggested itinerary that will help you make the most of your time in Tuscany:

8 Days Itinerary

Day 1: Arrival in Florence
- Arrive in Florence and check into your hotel.

- Take a walking tour of the city and explore some of its most famous landmarks such as the Duomo, Piazza della Signoria, and the Uffizi Gallery.

- Enjoy a great dinner of classic Tuscan food in one of the city's many eateries.

Day 2: Florence to Siena
- Take a train or drive to Siena, one of Tuscany's most picturesque hill towns.

- Explore the town's small alleyways, gorgeous piazzas, and historic buildings.

- Visit the Palazzo Pubblico, the town hall, and the Gothic Cathedral of Santa Maria Assunta.

- Enjoy a classic lunch of panino with porchetta (pork roast sandwich) and a glass of Chianti wine.

Day 3: Siena to San Gimignano
- Drive to San Gimignano, a lovely medieval hill town noted for its well-preserved towers.

- Visit the town's main square, Piazza della Cisterna, and the Church of Sant'Agostino.

- Take a guided tour of the town's historic core and learn about its history and cultural heritage.

- Enjoy a superb dinner of pasta with wild boar ragù (sauce) in one of the town's local trattorias.

Day 4: San Gimignano to Chianti
- Drive through the gorgeous countryside of the Chianti area and explore some of its picturesque villages and vineyards.

- Stop in Greve in Chianti to tour its historic town and try some of the local wines.

- Visit the hilltop village of Radda in Chianti, noted for its well-preserved medieval buildings and breathtaking views of the surrounding countryside.

- Have dinner at a typical agriturismo (farmhouse) and sample the local specialties, including wild boar stew and truffles.

Day 5: Chianti to Pienza
- Drive to Pienza, a picturesque hill town in the center of the Val d'Orcia, a UNESCO World Heritage Site.

- Explore the town's small alleyways, gorgeous piazzas, and Renaissance buildings.

- Visit the town's famed cathedral and the Palazzo Piccolomini, a Renaissance palace.

- Enjoy a picnic with pecorino cheese, prosciutto, and local wine in one of the town's lovely parks or gardens.

Day 6: Pienza to Montalcino
- Drive to Montalcino, a lovely hill town noted for its famous Brunello wine.

- Visit a local winery and try some of the region's best wines.

- Explore the town's medieval castle and historic center.

- Have dinner in one of the town's local trattorias and enjoy a traditional Tuscan feast.

Day 7: Montalcino to Lucca

- Drive to Lucca, a lovely medieval walled city that is recognized for its well-preserved ancient core.

- Visit the town's largest square, Piazza dell'Anfiteatro, and the Church of San Michele in Foro.

- Take a walk along the city's old walls, which give spectacular views of the town and its surroundings.

- Enjoy a gelato at one of the city's many gelaterias and explore its lovely alleys and alleyways.

- Have dinner in one of Lucca's famous trattorias and experience the local cuisine, including dishes cooked with olive oil, truffles, and porcini mushrooms.

Day 8: Departure from Florence

- Drive back to Florence and spend the day exploring the city's art and cultural treasures.

- Visit the Accademia Gallery to see Michelangelo's David.

- Take a trip around the lovely Boboli Gardens, located behind the Pitti Palace.

Enjoy a farewell dinner in one of the city's many wonderful restaurants before going back home.
This schedule is only a sample and can be altered to suit your unique interests and travel style.

2-Week Itinerary

A two-week plan will allow you to discover some of the most prominent tourist destinations and hidden jewels of this region. Here is a sample itinerary to help you make the most of your Tuscany vacation:

Day 1-2: Arrival in Florence

- Arrive in Florence, the capital of Tuscany, and check into your hotel. Spend the first two days visiting the city. Visit the Uffizi Gallery to witness some of the finest works of the Renaissance, such as Botticelli's "The Birth of Venus." Climb the stairs of the iconic Cathedral of Santa Maria del Fiore to experience amazing views of the city, and explore the stunning Piazza del Duomo. Stroll along the Ponte Vecchio, one of the oldest bridges in the city, and enjoy its bustling jewelry shops.

Day 3-4: Siena

- Take a short train ride to Siena. Visit the famed Piazza del Campo, the main plaza in Siena, and enjoy its stunning palaces and fountains. Explore the majestic Cathedral of Siena and its spectacular interior, which is filled with stunning murals and stained glass windows. Take a stroll through the small, twisting streets of the city and have a superb supper of authentic Tuscan food.

Day 5-6: Chianti

- Drive to Chianti, spend two days seeing this magnificent country, visiting fascinating ancient villages, and savoring the exquisite local wines. Take a picturesque trip along the Chiantigiana, a magnificent road that weaves through the rolling hills of the region, and stop at some of the tiny, family-run wineries to try their wines.

Day 7-8: San Gimignano

- Drive to San Gimignano, spend two days exploring this lovely town, visiting its many museums, churches, and palaces. Admire the breathtaking views of the surrounding countryside from the top of one of the town's famed towers, and meander through the tiny, twisting lanes of the city. Sample the great local cuisine and wines, and take a lovely drive over the undulating hills of the region.

Day 9-10: Pisa

- Drive to Pisa, and explore the famed Piazza dei Miracoli, home of the Leaning Tower, the Cathedral, and the Baptistery. Climb the stairs of the Leaning Tower for spectacular views of the city, and take a stroll around the gorgeous botanical gardens.

Day 11-12: Lucca

- Drive to Lucca, a picturesque city that is famed for its gorgeous walls, stunning cathedrals, and rich history. Spend two days here as well seeing this lovely city, and visiting its numerous museums, churches, and palaces. Take a walk around the city's famed walls, which give beautiful views of the surrounding countryside, and explore the stunning Cathedral of San Martino.

Day 13-14: Return to Florence

- Return to Florence and spend the remaining two days of your Tuscany holiday enjoying this magnificent city. Visit the famed Palazzo Pitti, home to one of the biggest collections of Renaissance art in the world, and take a stroll through the magnificent Boboli Gardens. Visit the famous Uffizi Gallery one more time, or visit the Accademia Gallery to see Michelangelo's iconic statue of David. Spend your last evening in Florence with a goodbye meal at a traditional Tuscan restaurant and eat some of the excellent local dishes and wines.

A two-week itinerary will allow you to discover some of the more popular destinations and hidden jewels of this gorgeous region.

3 weeks Itinerary

Here's a three-week itinerary for a thorough tour of Tuscany:

Week 1: Florence and its neighboring area

- Day 1: Arrive in Florence and check into your accommodation. Take a trip around the city center to acquire a sense of the city and its architecture. Visit the Cathedral of Santa Maria del Fiore, popularly known as the Florence Cathedral, and climb to the top for a panoramic view of the city.

- Day 2: Spend the day exploring the Uffizi Gallery, one of the world's oldest and most famous art museums. See masterpieces by painters such as Botticelli, da Vinci, and Michelangelo.

- Day 3: Visit the Accademia Gallery to see Michelangelo's famed statue of David. Take a walk around the Boboli Gardens, a magnificent area behind the Pitti Palace.

- Day 4: Take a day trip to the nearby town of Siena. This medieval town is noted for its Gothic architecture, particularly the beautiful Cathedral of Siena.

- Day 5-6: Spend two days touring the adjacent Chianti wine area, noted for its great wines and gorgeous countryside. Take a wine tour, visit local vineyards, and enjoy a lovely drive over the rolling hills.

Week 2: Southern Tuscany

- Day 7-8: Drive to Montepulciano, a magnificent hilltop town noted for its Renaissance architecture and wine industry. Take a tour of the town's cellars and sample some of the local wines.

- Day 9-10: Continue to Pienza, another magnificent hilltop town noted for its stunning

vistas and superb pecorino cheese. Visit local
cheese manufacturers and try the local cuisine.

- Day 11-12: Drive to the town of Montalcino,
  noted for its Brunello di Montalcino wine. Take a
  wine tour, visit local vineyards, and enjoy a
  picturesque drive through the countryside.

- Day 13-14: Drive to the town of Cortona, a
  delightful town famed for its tiny streets and
  breathtaking views. Explore the town's
  cathedrals, museums, and boutiques.

Week 3: Western'Tuscany

- Day 15-16: Drive to Lucca, a lovely walled city
  noted for its Renaissance architecture and
  gorgeous parks. Take a walk along the city's
  ramparts, visit the town's churches, and enjoy a
  bike ride through the town's parks.

- Day 17-18: Drive to the town of Viareggio, a
  seaside resort noted for its magnificent beaches
  and busy promenade. Spend the day lounging
  on the beach and exploring the town's shops and
  eateries.

- Day 19-20: Drive to the town of Cinque Terre, a
  collection of five stunning coastal towns noted for
  their rough shoreline and lovely villages. Take a

lovely trek along the coastline, visit local vineyards, and relax on the beaches.

- Day 21: Return to Florence and spend your last day visiting the city and shopping for mementos.

This itinerary includes the most attractive and intriguing aspects of Tuscany, including its major cities, lovely medieval towns, magnificent countryside, and coastline. By following this schedule, you will be able to enjoy the best of what Tuscany has to offer and develop memories that will last a lifetime.

Note: The order of towns can be modified to meet your schedule

Visiting Tuscany On a Budget

Visiting Tuscany on a budget is definitely achievable. Here are a few suggestions and tricks to help you make the most of your trip while keeping prices down.

Accommodation

- Stay in a guesthouse or bed & breakfast instead of a hotel. This can be a more economical choice, and it also allows you the opportunity to experience a more true, local atmosphere.

- Look for somewhere to stay outside the city center. Accommodations in the outskirts of Tuscany's major cities are often less expensive, and you can often find fantastic offers on rooms or flats that are only a short train or bus journey away from the city center.

- Consider a homestay or a holiday rental. Renting an apartment or staying with a local family can be a fantastic way to save money on accommodation prices, and it also gives a unique, authentic experience that you can't find in a hotel.

Food and drink

- Take advantage of the local markets. Tuscany is famed for its local goods, including cheeses, olive oil, and fresh fruit. You can get amazing bargains on these things at local markets, and you'll be able to sample the local flavors while saving money on your meals.

- Eat in local trattorias and osterias. These informal restaurants serve simple, delicious cuisine crafted using fresh, local ingredients. They're frequently less expensive than more upscale eateries, and you'll have a chance to experience the local cuisine.

- Drink local wine. Tuscany is one of Italy's most famous wine regions, and you can get good bottles of wine at local shops and markets for far less than you would pay in a restaurant.

Transportation

- Take the train. The train system in Tuscany is reliable, convenient, and economical. Trains connect the larger cities and many of the smaller communities, making it easy to move around without a car.

- Walk or bike. Many of Tuscany's cities and villages are small enough to explore on foot or by bike, and this is a fantastic way to save money on transportation costs while getting some exercise and seeing the sights.

- Consider automobile hire. If you want to explore the countryside or the less-touristed sections of Tuscany, consider renting a car. Just be aware that renting cars can be pricey, and driving in Italy can be tough, especially if you're not used to driving on tight, curving roads.

Sights and activities

- Visit free museums and galleries. Many museums and galleries in Tuscany offer free entrance or discounted admission rates on specific days of the week, so be sure to check before you visit.

- Take a walking tour. Many cities in Tuscany offer guided walking tours, which are a terrific opportunity to learn about the history and culture of the area.

- Explore the countryside. Tuscany is famous for its rolling hills, vineyards, and olive orchards, and there are many fantastic hikes and excursions to discover in the countryside.

- Visit the beaches. If you're visiting Tuscany in the summer, don't miss the chance to spend a day at the beach. There are numerous gorgeous beaches along the coast, and many of them are free to visit.

Tuscany is a fantastic destination, and there are numerous ways to travel on a budget. Whether you're interested in exploring

Getting Around

There are several possibilities for transportation to explore the area.

Here is a detailed explanation of the transportation alternatives available for moving throughout Tuscany:

Rail

- The train is a convenient and economical way to move about Tuscany, especially if you plan to travel between cities. The principal train station in Tuscany is Firenze Santa Maria Novella in Florence, which offers links to other cities in the region, including Pisa, Siena, and Lucca. The regional trains are called "Regionali" and are reasonably cheap, but not as fast as the high-speed trains.

Bus

- Bus travel is another economical alternative for moving to Tuscany. The regional bus operator, called "Busitalia," offers services connecting cities and communities in the region. Buses are a wonderful choice for accessing smaller settlements that are not accessible by train.

Car rental

- Renting a car is a simple method to see Tuscany, especially if you plan to visit distant villages or gorgeous countryside. There are many automobile rental firms in the major cities in Tuscany, including Florence, Pisa, and Siena. However, be advised that driving in Tuscany can be tough due to small roads and heavy traffic in some regions.

Taxi

- Taxis are readily available in Tuscany, especially in the larger cities, however, they can be fairly pricey compared to other kinds of transportation. Taxis can be hailed on the street or pre-booked with the "MyTaxi" app.

Bicycle

- Bicycle rental is a popular alternative for travelers who wish to discover Tuscany at their own leisure. Bicycle rental shops are generally available in the main cities, and many offer rental packages that include a bike, lock, and map. Bicycling is a terrific way to enjoy the picturesque countryside but be prepared for hills and windy roads.

Walking

- Walking is a fantastic method to discover Tuscany's cities and villages, especially in the ancient areas where cars are not allowed. Many cities, like Florence and Siena, have pedestrian-friendly streets, and walking is a delightful way to view the sights and drink up the local culture.

Shared Shuttle Bus Services

- For travelers who want to make the most of their stay in Tuscany, shared shuttle bus services are a practical and economical option. These services often pick up and drop off customers at their hotels or other designated areas and offer tours of the region's prominent monuments and attractive landscapes.

Tuscany offers a number of transportation alternatives to assist visitors to move around and see the region. Whether you prefer trains, buses, auto rentals, taxis, bicycles, walking, or shared shuttle bus services, Tuscany has something to offer for everyone. Choose the transportation option that best fits your travel style and budget, and enjoy your trip to Tuscany.

Shopping for Souvenirs

Shopping for souvenirs in Tuscany is an opportunity to bring back memories and unique things from one of the most famous regions of Italy. When shopping for souvenirs in Tuscany, you will find a wide choice of things that showcase the region's traditional arts and crafts. Here is a detailed overview of what you may expect when shopping for souvenirs in Tuscany.

Leather goods

- Tuscany is famed for its leather goods, and Florence is particularly noted for its high-quality leather. You may find a large choice of leather products, including bags, wallets, belts, shoes, and coats. Most of these things are handmade, and the leather is of the best quality. Look for the "Made in Italy" logo when shopping for leather products in Tuscany.

Pottery

- This region's pottery is recognized for its traditional style, high quality, and unique designs. Deruta and Montelupo Fiorentino are two of the most notable centers for Tuscan pottery production. You may get a large choice of ceramic products, including plates, bowls, vases, and mugs. These objects are commonly adorned with the distinctive blue and yellow motifs that are so characteristic of Tuscan ceramics.

Wine and Olive Oil

- Tuscany is known for its wine and olive oil, and both make fantastic keepsakes for those who enjoy the finer things in life. You may purchase a large choice of wine and olive oil goods in Tuscany, including bottles of Chianti, Brunello di Montalcino, and other notable Tuscan wines. You can also get a variety of olive oil products, including flavored oils, cold-pressed oils, and infused oils.

Jewelry

- Tuscany is also famed for its jewelry, and you can discover a wide choice of jewelry products in the region, including gold, silver, and valuable gemstones. Florence is particularly known for its jewelry, and you can find a range of jewelry boutiques in the city that offer unique and high-quality products.

Clothing

- Tuscan clothing is recognized for its style and craftsmanship. You can buy a variety of apparel products in Tuscany, including typical Tuscan garments, such as the classic linen shirt and the colorful scarf. You can also find a choice of different clothing options, like leather coats, suede shoes, and hand-knit sweaters.

Food

- Tuscany is famous for its cuisine, and you may purchase a large choice of food goods to take home as mementos. Look for local specialties, such as truffles, cured meats, and cheeses. You may also buy a variety of food products, such as sauces, oils, and vinegar, that are produced with traditional Tuscan ingredients.

Art

- Tuscany is famed for its art, and you can discover a wide choice of art products in the region. Look for traditional Tuscan paintings, such as those by Botticelli and Michelangelo, as well as current Tuscan painters. You may also find a variety of other art objects, such as sculptures, ceramics, and prints.

Souvenir shops

- There are many souvenir shops in Tuscany, where you may purchase a wide choice of products that reflect the region's traditional arts and crafts. You can find these shops throughout the cities and towns of Tuscany, as well as in the countryside. Many of these shops sell handmade things, and you can often find unique and one-of-a-kind items that are not available anywhere else.

Markets

- Another fantastic spot to purchase souvenirs in Tuscany is in the local markets. You may find a wide selection of things at the markets, including food, clothing, jewelry, and art. The markets are a terrific place to find unique and affordable souvenirs, and you can often haggle pricing with the merchants. Some of the most notable markets in Tuscany include the San Lorenzo Market in Florence, the Mercato Centrale in Florence, and the Mercato di Sant'Ambrogio in Florence.

Where to buy

- When shopping for souvenirs in Tuscany, you can find a wide choice of products in the cities and towns of the region, as well as in the countryside. Some of the most prominent cities for shopping in Tuscany include Florence, Pisa, Siena, and Lucca. In these cities, you can discover a large choice of souvenir stores, markets, and other locations to buy things.

Tips for buying souvenirs in Tuscany

Be mindful of false things

- Be careful when shopping for souvenirs in Tuscany, as there are many fake products accessible in the region. To prevent buying fake products, search for the "Made in Italy" label and only purchase things from recognized retailers or markets.

Negotiate prices

- In Tuscany, it is normal to negotiate prices, especially in the markets. Be prepared to bargain a bit to get the best deal.

Buy local items

- To enjoy the most real Tuscan experience, try to buy local products, such as those manufactured by local artists.

Take your time

- Shopping for souvenirs in Tuscany is a terrific opportunity to take your time and appreciate the region's rich history, art, and culture. Don't feel rushed and take the time to pick the right mementos for you and your loved ones.

Shopping for souvenirs in Tuscany is a unique and pleasurable experience that allows you to bring back memories and unique presents from one of the most famous regions of Italy. From leather items and pottery to wine and olive oil, you will find a wide choice of products that showcase the region's traditional arts and crafts.

Tour Package Options

There are various tour packages available for travelers to Tuscany, offering a range of activities, from cultural and historical tours to food and wine tastings. Here are some of the popular tour package options for travelers visiting Tuscany:

Cultural and historical tours: These tours are great for individuals interested in learning about the region's rich history and culture. Visitors can explore Tuscany's cities and villages, visit museums and galleries, and view iconic monuments, such as the Leaning Tower of Pisa, the Cathedral of Santa Maria del Fiore in Florence, and the Roman amphitheater at Pula.

Food and wine tours: Tuscany is recognized for its wonderful cuisine and world-renowned wines, and many trip packages are focused on this part of the region's culture. Visitors can visit local vineyards, eat local foods, and learn about the region's food and wine traditions.

Art and architecture tours: Tuscany is also recognized for its cultural past, and visitors can take tours to see the region's famed art and architectural marvels, such as the works of Michelangelo, Botticelli, and Leonardo da Vinci.

Outdoor activities: Tuscany is famed for its natural beauty, and visitors may explore the countryside and enjoy outdoor activities, such as hiking, cycling, and horseback riding. Many travel packages provide options for outdoor activities, such as guided walks and bike trips.

Customizable tours: For those who prefer a more personalized experience, there are various tour operators who provide customizable tours, allowing travelers to construct their own itinerary and choose which cities and sights to visit.

Luxury tours: Tuscany is a favorite destination for luxury travelers, and there are various tour operators that offer opulent vacation packages, including high-end lodgings, private tours, and gourmet meals.

When picking a tour package for Tuscany, it is crucial to consider your budget, hobbies, and the length of time you have available. It is also a good idea to book early in advance, as many tour companies fill up quickly during the peak travel season.

There are numerous tour package options available, so guests can choose the tour that best meets their interests and budget. Booking a tour package is a terrific way to make the most of your stay in Tuscany, ensuring that you see all the attractions and experience all the finest the region has to offer.

If you're interested in a Tour package, I recommend visiting the website stated in the link below, as they provide a vast range of possibilities for whatever vacation experience you have in mind while arranging your trip, and also you may book tours proportionally to your budget.

Resources

You can still use the TravelAdisor App to arrange a tour of your choice.

/

Check the websites below for other potential options:
https://www.zicasso.com/luxury-tours/italy/tuscany/vacation-package

/

Musement.com

Tourist Safety Tips

While Tuscany is generally a safe area to visit, it's crucial to be aware of potential hazards and to take appropriate steps to guarantee a safe and happy journey.

Utilize licensed and trustworthy transportation providers: When looking for transportation in Tuscany, make sure to use licensed and reputable organizations, you may also use the Busitalia we mentioned.

Avoid illegal taxi drivers: Unlicensed taxi drivers can be dangerous and may overcharge you or take you to unsafe regions. If you need a taxi, utilize the MyTaxi app.

Be wary of pickpocketing: Pickpocketing is a widespread problem in tourist places. Keep your belongings near to your body and be especially cautious in busy settings.

Use caution when using ATMs: Use ATMs located in well-lit, public areas and be mindful of your surroundings when withdrawing money.

Avoid walking alone at night: It is usually recommended to avoid wandering alone at night, especially in unknown places. If you must walk alone, make careful to stay in well-lit places and be mindful of your surroundings.

Keep a low profile: Try to avoid wearing expensive jewelry or carrying significant quantities of cash. This will help to lessen the chance of theft.

Use a money belt or travel pouch: A money belt or travel pouch might help to keep your valuables safe while you are out and about.

Stay informed: Keep up-to-date with local news and developments, especially if there are any safety issues or advisories in the area you are visiting.

Know your route: Make sure you know the path you are traveling before you start your journey. This will enable you to keep on track and prevent getting lost.

Be prepared for emergencies: Make sure you have a fully charged mobile phone with you and keep emergency numbers on hand.

Respect local conventions and laws: Familiarize yourself with local customs and laws before you travel. This will allow you to avoid breaching the law and offending local neighbors.

Have travel insurance: Make sure you have travel insurance in case of accidents, theft, or illness.

Use public transit: Using public transportation helps to lower your carbon footprint and encourages sustainable travel.

Respect local wildlife: Tuscany is home to a variety of wildlife, therefore it is crucial to respect their habitats and avoid disturbing them.

Respect local architecture and landmarks: Tuscany is abundant in old structures and landmarks, thus it is crucial to respect these and not destroy them in any manner.

Support local businesses: By shopping at local markets and eating at local restaurants, you can support the local economy and help to maintain the region's unique cultural history.

Be careful of littering: Littering can have a harmful influence on the environment, so make sure to dispose of your rubbish correctly.

Finally, it is crucial to have a cheerful attitude and an open mind when vacationing in Tuscany. By approaching the journey with a spirit of inquiry and respect, you will be able to completely enjoy the beauty and culture of this beautiful place.

In conclusion, Tuscany is a safe and delightful area to visit. By taking a few easy precautions, you may ensure that your trip is pleasurable and stress-free. By using licensed and reputable transportation companies, being aware of pickpocketing, using caution when using ATMs, avoiding walking alone at night, keeping a low profile, using a money belt or travel pouch, staying informed, knowing your route, being prepared for emergencies, respecting local customs and laws, and having travel insurance, you can ensure that your trip to Tuscany is safe and memorable.

Festival and Culture

Tuscany region organizes several festivals and events throughout the year. Here are some of the popular ones in Tuscany:

Florence International Artisan Fair (Fiera Internazionale dell'Artigianato): Held in Florence every year in the month of April, this festival highlights the best of Tuscan and Italian workmanship. From leather items and ceramics to jewelry and textiles, the fair is a celebration of the traditional crafts of the region.

Lucca Summer Festival: This festival is held in July in the city of Lucca, and is one of the most important music events in Italy. The festival has a mix of foreign and local musicians and is a terrific opportunity to experience live music in a lovely location.

Carnival of Viareggio: This celebration is celebrated in February and is one of the largest and most famous carnivals in Italy. It contains colorful floats, costumed entertainers, and plenty of food and music.

Olive Oil Festival (Festa dell'Olio): Held in December in the town of Impruneta, this festival commemorates the production of olive oil in Tuscany. The festival contains food, wine, and of course, plenty of olive oil for guests to experience.

Florence International Fashion Week: Held in February, this event is one of the most major fashion events in Italy. The week offers collections from some of the most outstanding designers in the world and is a terrific opportunity for fashion aficionados to view the latest trends and designs.

Palio di Siena: This horse race is held twice a year, in July and August, in the city of Siena. It is a stunning event that dates back to the Middle Ages and is one of the most famous and ancient festivals in Tuscany.

Pienza Cheese Festival (Festa del Formaggio di Pienza): Held in September, this festival commemorates the manufacturing of Pecorino cheese in the town of Pienza. The festival involves cheese samples, cooking demos, and plenty of local food and wine.

Arezzo Wave Love Event: This festival is held in July in Arezzo and is one of the major independent music festivals in Italy. The festival showcases a mix of local and international musicians and is a terrific opportunity to explore new and rising music talent.

Cortona On the Move: This festival is held in July in the town of Cortona and is one of the largest photography events in Italy. The festival comprises exhibitions, workshops, and events dedicated to the art of photography.

Tuscan Sun Event: This festival is celebrated in July in Cortona and is a celebration of music, food, wine, and culture. The festival showcases performances by some of the top local and international performers and is a terrific opportunity to explore the rich culture and traditions of Tuscany.

Siena Jazz Festival: Held in July, this festival is one of the largest and most prominent jazz festivals in Italy. The festival showcases a mix of local and international musicians and is a terrific opportunity to hear live jazz music in a lovely environment.

Florence Biennale: This biennial event is hosted in Florence and is one of the largest exhibitions of contemporary art in Italy. The Biennale comprises exhibitions and events related to contemporary art and is a terrific opportunity to explore new and rising artists and trends.

Sagra Delle Cantine: This festival is held in September and celebrates the production of wine in Tuscany. The festival takes place in several towns and villages throughout the region and offers wine tastings, food, and live music.

Tuscany is also home to various historic events, such as the Calcio Storico Fiorentino, a historic soccer tournament that has been hosted in Florence since the

16th century. The competition is a unique and entertaining event that is not to be missed.

In conclusion, Tuscany is an area rich in culture and history and holds several festivals and events throughout the year. Whether you are interested in music, gastronomy, fashion, art, or history, Tuscany has something to offer everyone. So, organize your trip today and explore the rich culture and customs of this wonderful region.

Printed in Great Britain
by Amazon